MW01699946

Musk
Gango

by

Mary Burpee

Clarence Burpee and musk oxen of Gango

BOREALIS

Borealis Press
Ottawa, Canada
2002

Copyright © by Mary J. Burpee
and Borealis Press Ltd., 2002

All rights reserved. No part of this book may be used or reproduced in any manner whatsoever without prior written permission from the Publisher, except in the case of brief quotations embodied in critical articles and reviews.

Canadä

We acknowledge the financial assistance of the Government of Canada through the Book Publishing Program (BPIDP) for our publishing activities.

National Library of Canada Cataloguing in Publication Data

Burpee, Mary J. (Mary Josephine), 1918-
Musk oxen of Gango

ISBN-0-88887-202-X

1. Muskox farming. I. Title.

SF401.M8B87 2002 C2002-900308-3

Cover design by Bull's Eye Design, Ottawa, Canada

Photographs by Mary J. Burpee and others.

Printed and bound in Canada on acid free paper.

Table of Contents

Illustrations

Acknowledgements

To J.S. Tener for his scientific book entitled *Muskoxen* which provided information about the physical aspects of musk oxen and the conditions in which they lived in the Arctic.

To David R. Gray for his book entitled *Status of Musk Oxen on Canadian Arctic Islands*.

To Peter Mathhiesen for his book *Oomingmak* explaining how wild calves can be captured.

To Bernhard Grzimek for his book *Wild Animal White Man* giving information on the way elk have been used as work animals.

Thank you to Al Oeming, Paul Wilkinson, and Dee McConnell for the verbal information they gave my husband about their experiences with musk oxen.

Chapter 1

The New Musk-ox Calf

"Get her out of here before she dies. She's your responsibility now." Those words did little to lessen the concerns of a man trying to flesh out a dream so new the world had no concept of what he was attempting to achieve.

Now it was scarcely five hours later.

"Hurry! Shut the gate. I want to let her out of the crate." The words cut through the crisp December air the way a razor-sharp knife slices carrots.

Sixteen-year old Rod moved quickly to help Grandpa shift the heavy plank gate into position and fasten it with a stout chain. I clambered over the corral fence and into the make-shift barn. I didn't want to miss anything.

The crate had just been unloaded from our half-ton truck. The animal inside alternated between glaring at the world from eyes big as balloons, and bashing her brains against the front of the crate. The crate was strong, and well padded. Built especially to hold a six-month old musk oxen calf, but one wondered how long it could survive such maniacal charges.

When she charged it was in salvos of three. As if whatever triggered her attack mechanism was programmed for three head-bashing volleys without a moment's respite. Despite the heavy padding on the planks her forehead was bloody, the hairs matted.

I began to have concerns about the wisdom of this venture, then immediately remembered the musk oxen I'd seen at Fairbanks, Alaska. They had been quiet and friendly. Even the cows had come up to be petted. So it must be the trauma of being separated from her mother, shoved into a crate, and taken on a long truck ride that was upsetting Musky.

The trip from the Calgary Zoo to what would be the musk ox's new home at Gango Ranch, near Hughenden, in east central Alberta, hadn't been a fun trip for my husband, Clarence, and son, Rod, either. Musky had kicked up such a ruckus at finding herself in the crate that Zoo Manager, Bill McKay, had quickly waved them on their way growling "Get her out of here before she dies. She's your responsibility now."

As they drove those words played over and over in my husband's mind like a phonograph needle stuck in the groove of a warped record. It did nothing to dispel concerns for a man starting down a path no one had walked before. The significance of McKay's parting words were intensified by the continuous din from the crate behind.

Clarence and Rod drove in silence. They knew adult musk oxen from the wilds can never be tamed. If caught they fight confinement until exhaustion leads to death. Yet very young calves quickly imprint on man and accept him as both meal ticket and friend.

At the moment six-month old Musky seemed to have taken on the behavior pattern of an adult.

As the noises in the crate behind gradually subsided Clarence breathed easier. She was finally settling down.

Then Rod's anxious voice shattered the silence. "Dad. What's wrong with the truck? It's vibrating. And there's a thumping sound. Can't you hear it?"

Clarence, who had been half dozing as sixteen-year-old Rod drove, listened, his ears attuned for motor trouble, then he gave a low gasp. "I think it's her heart we're hearing."

"What'll we do?" Rod nervously moistened his lips, his voice brittle with anxiety.

"Pull over and stop."

But when they did the musk oxen started throwing herself around again. Not knowing what else to do they got back into the cab and kept driving. Although the ruckus gradually stopped, the heavy pounding of her heart did not.

Rod tried to relieve the tension in the cab by punctuating the passing miles with “She isn’t dead yet Dad. Her heart’s still pounding.”

Chapter Two

Back at the Ranch

Meanwhile back at the ranch there were chores to be done and I had elected to stay home and do them. However it was hard to keep my mind off the truck and its occupants. Where were they now? What were they doing? In 1971 there were no cell phones. No way to keep in contact with the travelers.

With the thermometer hugging thirty-five degrees below zero Fahrenheit, my first morning chore was lighting the heater in the stock tank. Already the water had a thick coating of ice. I automatically shoved paper, kindling and wood into the tank heater as I'd often seen my husband do, and struck a match. It flickered and went out. So did a second and a third as they too were caught in a draft of cold air that sucked away their life. My fingers were getting numb.

Carefully I struck a fourth match and shielded it with my mittened hand. This time the flame grabbed eagerly at the crumpled pages of last week's *Western Producer*, and ran up it, flaming and crackling, reaching first for the kindling and then the wood. Soon the fire was roaring up the old tin stovepipe and smoke rose in a straight thin column, then lost itself in the rosy glow of coming dawn. I watched it and wondered.

Would my husband's dream of domesticating musk oxen be like the smoke and fade into nothingness?

I thought of the events leading up to this day. It began in 1958 when Clarence read a *Readers' Digest* article about musk oxen. An experimental herd of six had been captured as calves in 1954 from the Thelon Game Reserve in the heart of the North West Territories by an American named John Teal, and taken to his farm in Vermont.

Early Arctic explorers had labelled musk oxen "fierce and cantankerous, the most dangerous of all game animals"; but John Teal said his six were easily the tamest animals on the farm.

That article sparked my husband's interest. From then on he studied everything he could find about musk oxen. Which wasn't much. And what there was had a certain similarity.

Most writers agreed that musk oxen, shaggy survivors of the last ice age, were well designed to withstand the intense cold and scanty food of the high Arctic. All mentioned their unique method of defence.

The herd's rumps-in-heads-out formation serves them well when attacked by wolves, their worst natural enemy. It presents a formidable wall of wickedly slashing horns that few predators care to challenge.

But for men with guns it is a set-up for slaughter. Entire herds can be shot with almost no effort. When one falls kicking spasmodically, its life-blood staining the snow, the rest close rank and wait for a similar fate. It's a sickening sight in which there is no sport. A massacre to make strong men turn away in disgust.

The under-wool of the musk oxen, known by its Eskimo name, qiviut, is a remarkable fiber. According to tests done at Leeds University by Dr. Farrer Barker, it is finer then cashmere, wears like merino, and will not shrink even when washed in hot water. It was this coupled with the animals' ability to thrive on sparse Arctic ranges that made my husband believe they warranted a place in agriculture.

The more he learned about this singular northern animal the more enthusiastic he became. But few others shared his interest and for years Governments blocked all attempts to keep musk oxen outside of zoos. However by

1970 their policy changed. Now anyone holding a restricted-game farm licence could keep musk oxen.

Unfortunately my husband still faced a very major problem. There were no musk oxen.

No, that's not quite right.

There were wild herds in the North, some of them facing almost certain starvation on overstocked Arctic islands. Yet permission to buy doomed calves and ship them to a southern utopia was denied. That left established zoos as the only source of musk ox calves, and they rarely had any to sell.

So in late 1971 when Clarence learned the Calgary Zoo had a heifer calf they would sell, (the price seemed exorbitant, but what the heck) he was walking on air. A dream of thirteen years was about to be born. But first he had to prepare a place for the animal, and then get the licence required to keep it.

A warm body snuggling against my leg, a head pushing under my mittened hand brought me out of my thoughts. It was Rev, our German Shepherd, reminding me if I had nothing better to do than stand and stare into space I might as well pay some attention to her. I patted her absently, threw another chunk of wood on the tank-heater and turned away.

She frisked around me like a puppy as I trudged off through the snow to open a gate. Together we stood aside and watched as the hungry cows streamed through, impatient to get to the feed Clarence had put out for them the day before.

Turning to go I heard the barn door slam and knew Terry Lee, home from University for the Christmas vacation, had finished the horse chores.

Khem reared and whinnied when I passed the stallion pen, then pranced over to greet me. I stroked his velvety muzzle wondering if I'd ever be doing that to a musk ox.

Terry Lee joined me and we walked together towards

the house. Behind us the sunrise was turning the eastern sky into a blazing inferno. Did it portend a coming storm? Involuntarily I shuddered and as if by common consent we started to run.

The kitchen felt warm and welcoming with its tantalizing aromas of bacon and coffee. All my forbodings were temporarily forgotten in the buzz of talk that is inevitable when a family gets together.

Heather and her husband, John Lea, had arrived the night before from Fairview. Grannie and Grandpa Kennedy had come from Camrose on Boxing Day. Only Clarence and Rod were missing. But our thoughts were with them.

Were they on their way home? Or still trying to get the calf separated from its mother and into a crate?

A musk ox defending her calf is not something one wants to mess around with. Massive horns that end in rapier-sharp points arc downward in long sweeping curves. They can disembowel a wolf with one swipe. Why not a man?

Suddenly I wished I had never heard John Teal's remark. "If a musk oxen is out to get you, there is no way he's not going to succeed." The day grew grey and closed in around me as more morbid thoughts crowded my brain.

What if the musk oxen smashed the crate and broke out? Or what if the truck skidded on the icy roads and upset?

Immediately my hands felt clammy as another grisly thought elbowed its way into my brain. A friend's stallion, a frequent campaigner, had dropped dead in the trailer enroute to a show. "Shock" the veterinarians called it. And then there was our neighbour involved in a minor motor accident. Shock, not injuries, had killed her too. Couldn't shock kill a musk ox?

My thoughts plummeted back to earth when John asked. "How are the calves doing Mum? Any trouble with pneumonia or shipping fever? I hear some ranchers are losing quite a few this year."

"No. . . ." and my mind raced off on another tangent. If calves, after centuries of domestication, still died of shipping fever, why not a musk ox? For an animal as wild as the winds that swoop and howl across the top of the world, pneumonia loomed as a grave danger.

What little information there was about musk oxen seemed to indicate that while they could be subject to similar maladies as cattle, they might also respond to the same treatments. But on the other hand it could take years of trial and error before serums suitable for musk oxen could be perfected. In the meantime how many would die?

"That is quite a corral Mum. It looks strong enough to hold an elephant." Heather's voice coming from the sewing room jarred me back to reality. "You built it in two weeks?" She sounded incredulous. Heather having scraped frost off the window was looking at the new corral north of the house through a tiny frost-free spot the size of a quarter.

John joined her and got his eye to the peep-hole. After a moment he exclaimed. "Wow! That's high enough for a giraffe. What is it? Six feet?"

"Nope! Seven." Terry Lee's voice had a triumphant ring as she came from the kitchen, a tea-towel still in her hand.

"Why did you put the four bottom planks tight together, then leave six-inch spaces between the other four?" Heather has a teacher's curiosity for detail.

"Lee McConnell, manager of the musk oxen in Fairbanks, advised us to do it that way. It's supposed to prevent the musk ox from trying to climb out. He says they'll attempt to climb anything they can get a hind foot up on."

"I'm proud of that fence" Terry Lee's blue eyes were

sparkling like snow diamonds glittering under a full moon. “Did you notice it’s built in sections and hinged together? That’s so it can be easily taken apart and moved when the musk ox needs fresh pasture.”

“Too bad you didn’t come sooner John.” Terry Lee grinned as she glanced at her brother-in-law. “Then you could have helped to build it too. Everyone else did. Daddy and Rod sawed planks and welded iron bars into hinges. I drilled holes, Mum put in bolts and tightened nuts. When Grandpa came he was out helping too as soon as he got into what he calls his working clothes.

“Would you believe we worked on those gates Christmas Eve, with the temperature outside at fifty below? We probably set some sort of record. Maybe it ought to make the Guinness’s *Book of Records*.”

“Wasn’t it too cold?” Heather wanted to know.

“Not really. We built them in the shop. It’s heated. Anyway we were too excited about getting a musk ox to let a little cold bother us.”

“Fifty below. Some “little cold.” John grimaced and turned away.

“Nothing like a musk ox for family togetherness,” I thought wryly as I hurried to finish peeling the potatoes before joining the children at the window.

I didn’t need to look through the peep-hole to know that beyond that window, in the shelter of a poplar bluff, stood a new musk-ox corral, holding within its borders one gnarled old tree, a few saplings, a broken off stump, some scrub undergrowth, and a bit of last summer’s grass poking its weary head above the snow to wave dejectedly in the winter wind.

It seemed hard to believe it was only yesterday morning I had watched the corral take shape. Now it seemed eons since I had admired Clarence’s skill at maneuvering churchill, the custom-made front-end-loader, into difficult corners. With practised precision he swung the gates, one by one, into the exact position and Rod quickly hinged them together by dropping in a bolt and tightening a nut.

The six gates made a hexagon-shaped corral with a barn at one end. The title "barn" seemed to flatter the little old granary, unpainted and grey, that had been strongly reinforced and pressed into service until there was time to build something better. But we had gone to the trouble of putting in a window, nine feet above the ground. Musk oxen are good jumpers, we weren't taking any chances.

Inside the barn was what Clarence termed a 'training pen'. It was a stoutly built cubicle too high for me to see over unless I climbed up on a bale. It was just wide enough for a musk ox to stand or lie down in comfortably, but not turn around. Or so we thought.

Our plans for taming musk ox calves hinged on this training pen. We had seen similar ones used at the musk ox farm at Fairbanks, and they appeared to work well.

Was it only yesterday that I had hurried my husband and son on their way, knowing that to reach Calgary before the early dark of winter, they best get going? As they drove away the half-ton truck was almost hidden by eddying snow and exhaust. I breathed a prayer for their safety.

Now, barely twenty-four hours later I was watching for their return.

Beyond the kitchen window the land was bleak and cold and forbidding. Snow devils chased each other relentlessly across the yard before piling into weird hoodoo shapes. All the world seemed dull and flat and grey, the horizon drifting into the sky. And still no sign of the truck.

The afternoon was getting progressively stormier. Drifts kept sifting and swirling, growing deeper and deeper. Grannie sorting through a pile of Rod's work-socks to see which ones needed darning, wondered anxiously if the pick-up could get through them. Grandpa reassured her and announced cheerfully, "I'm looking for them anytime now."

It was 2.30.

To be doing something, anything, I began straightening the jumble of snow boots thrown carelessly onto the porch floor. Before I finished someone yelled excitedly "Here they come!"

That triggered a rush to struggle into winter clothing, tugging on boots, tying scarves, fastening parka-hoods, snatching up mittens without caring whose they were. Everyone was anxious to see the musk ox.

Suddenly a feeling of near panic swept over me. There were so many things that could have gone wrong.

One doesn't live with a man for twenty-five years without knowing how he ticks, so with a heart racing like a motor with a broken governor I looked through the partially-frosted porch window. A tiny suggestion of a smile was playing hide-and-seek across my husband's face. I opened the door and went out.

A young female musk ox (Kivy's calf Esky)

Chapter Three

Musky's Wild Arrival

The young musk ox, feeling completely abandoned by her own kind, watched us through the bars of the crate with eyes wild with fear. Her quivering muscles and thumping heart signalled her terror. Intending to soothe her as I would a frightened foal, I squatted on my haunches to reach in and pet her—then did a credible version of a backward summersault. The calf had snorted, stamped, and lunged at me. Her head slammed into the front of the crate, hitting it three times with trip-hammer precision. She stopped a moment, backed up swinging her head slowly from side to side, then went at it again. I looked at her with ballooning concern. I hoped when she was out of the crate and into the more roomy training pen she would feel less threatened.

However, getting her out of the crate and into the pen wasn't the simple matter Clarence had expected. Ordinarily when one raises an end-gate the animal inside backs out. Musky didn't. Or wouldn't.

When she heard the men behind her trying to raise the end-gate she flew back, ramming her rear-end into it, jamming it so it wouldn't open. When they tried to push her ahead, she pushed back harder.

Was it possible she connected the sound of the end-gate dropping with being caught? And now when sounds behind her suggested freedom she couldn't wait?

Whether or not that was so, she finally eased ahead and Clarence was able to yank up the end-gate. Instantly the heifer shot backwards and didn't stop backing until her hind-end was tight against the far end of the training pen.

John barely had time to slam the pen door shut before she hurtled ahead, hitting the door three times with deadly precision.

Yikes! We might think our musk ox was home. But it was enemy territory to her.

The sound of voices, movement of any kind triggered new explosions. When I climbed onto an upturned box to get a better look at her she sprang at me like a striking rattlesnake, her front feet knifing murderously close to my face.

Heather thought it politic to look at her from behind. The musk ox reared, pivoted, and charged her.

That shook us. A musk ox wasn't supposed to be able to turn in a two-foot wide training pen. We had built ours to Fairbanks specifications . . . wide enough for their musk ox to stand in or lie down, but not wide enough for them to turn around. Our musk ox had just done the supposedly impossible.

We had counted on the training pen as a place to quieten her, reasoning if she couldn't turn around it would be safe to go into the pen with her. A musk ox's head can be deadly but all one had to do was stay out of its reach and you'd be OK. Now it was obvious that would be impossible. How many more miss-assumptions had we made?

"Here's a pail of water Dad. Maybe she's thirsty." Terry Lee always thoughtful of animals, had brought it from the house.

Clarence took it and trying not to alarm Musky began to slowly lower it into the pen. The musk ox lunged, hitting the pail a home-run crack that sent it sailing out of her pen looking as if it had been run over by a freight train. Water droplets sprayed over everything, freezing as they hit.

Even though the pail was gone Musky kept bashing

her head against the door.

When those ructions finally subsided Clarence dropped a wisp of hay into the pen hoping she might eat it. But again she charged, hitting the hay and scattering it before it had time to reach the floor, and then it was back to charging the door again.

How much more of this could the door take? I looked at Clarence anxiously.

"I'm getting out of here," muttered Heather. "I don't want to be around if she gets out."

Her Dad smiled a tiny half-smile and said quietly "I don't think you need worry. That's a stout pen. But perhaps we ought to leave her alone now. Give her time to settle down."

Looking at my husband's broad shoulders I wondered again about the wisdom of this venture. Where his shoulders broad enough to carry such a big challenge? And pondering this I went with the others to the house.

A musk ox-family

Chapter Four

A Brief History of Musk Oxen

The drive home from Calgary had been filled with tension and doubts. But now relaxing over coffee and fresh cinnamon buns Clarence was eager to tell John what he had learned about the animals that had sparked his interest more than a decade ago.

"Zoologists in the nineteenth century believed they had identified several musk oxen sub-species. Today it appears there are really only two: Ovibos m. wardi, the so-called white-faced musk ox of Greenland and the Arctic Islands of Canada, and Ovibos m. moschatus, the larger, barren-land animal of the Western Arctic mainland. There is so little genetic difference in these two species that if they breed together their offspring are fertile."

"But haven't I read somewhere that during Pleistocene times there were other musk oxen? Extinct now of course. Probably contemporaries of animals like the hairy mammoth" Heather was thumbing through the pages of J. S Tener's book *Muskoxen* with a teacher's interest.

"Yes, you're right. The most noteworthy among them appears to be the Giant musk oxen. I understand its bones can still be found buried in the banks of frozen river beds in the high Arctic."

"Mercy! Imagine anyone wanting to go way up there just to find bones." Grannie shivered, then quickly poured herself another cup of tea. It was as if the thought of digging for bones in frozen tundra was making her chilly.

Now my husband was speaking again. "Since Henry Kelsey first saw musk oxen in 1689 a lot has been written and told about them. I imagine most of it could be classed as hearsay. It was largely their inaccessible habitat that led to musk oxen being regarded as almost legendary monsters from the last ice age, about to become extinct themselves. And therefore of no lasting importance.

“In prehistoric times musk oxen, along with the woolly mammoth, the saber-tooth tiger and Cro-Magnon man roamed over much of North America, as well as parts of Europe. Their bones have been found as far south as Kentucky , Arkansas, and Texas as well as in England, France, Germany, Norway, Russia and Siberia.”

“Yes Dad, and I know an archeology student who has spoken of a small, brooch-like artifact, believed to date from before the time of Christ. It was unearthed at an archeological dig near Urg in Northern Mongolia. He says it has such a striking likeness to our present day musk oxen he believes they must also have lived in Asia.”

“No reason why they shouldn’t, Terry Lee.” Grandpa was rubbing his hand thoughtfully over his chin as he spoke “If musk ox bones have been discovered in Siberia isn’t it logical to assume they would also have roamed over much of Mongolia? Maybe Tibet too?”

“Haven’t I heard that Musk oxen disappeared from Europe after the last ice-age? If so they probably escaped annihilation in North America because they were able to follow the melting glaciers northward. I suppose they were such easy targets, even for prehistoric hunters, that only those that moved to a barren, inhospitable land survived.”

”You’re quite right John. When harassed, musk oxen do became tragically easy to kill. Instead of running from an enemy they whirl to defend themselves. Massed together they stand shoulder to shoulder stamping and snorting. Some nervously rub their nose on an extended foreleg; others make short abortive charges before backing into the safety of the group again. But basically they all wait, like victims facing a firing squad, while hunters walk to within a few yards before starting their grisly slaughter. At such point-blank range few bullets fail to find their mark.

"Even men with primitive weapons had little trouble killing musk oxen. Dogs were frequently used to distract a herd while hunters sneaked close enough to drive their lances into the animals.

"Sometimes, in order to break up the menacing wall of horns facing him, an Eskimo would attach a thong to a rock and throw it over the animals' backs, then pull it towards him. This caused such panic and confusion among the musk oxen that animals could easily be speared with almost no danger to the hunter.

"Man, together with a harsh climate, almost succeeded in annihilating musk oxen from the face of the earth. Did you know that in the last half of the nineteenth century avaricious fur companies encouraged the slaughter of entire herds? They saw it as the most expeditious way to get hides quickly and easily. Records kept during that period indicate fifteen-thousand musk ox skins were brought in by hunters and whalers. The massacre reached its gory peak in 1890 when over sixteen-hundred hides were traded."

Grannie clucked sympathetically, then jabbed her darning needle viciously into a skein of wool as if she might fancy doing that to one of the hunters.

"Up until the 1880s the only interest in musk oxen was their hides and meat. Then a new market began to surface. Zoological gardens became interested in getting calves.

"Most of the calves were caught along the coast of Greenland by whalers who made a practice of shooting all the adults in order to safely get even one calf. It is estimated 2,000 adults were killed in Greenland to capture as few as 225 calves. Sadly most of the calves died of stress and improper food before they reached their destination.

Few survived to maturity.

"Finally zoological gardens, realizing their interest was endangering the species, refused to buy any more. By this time musk oxen were on the verge of extinction.

"In 1917 public sentiment prompted the Canadian Government to pass legislation to protect the musk oxen. In 1927 they set up a sixteen-thousand square mile sanctuary known as the Thelon Game Reserve deep in the heart of the North West Territories. With only about 500 animals left in the Canadian Arctic from which to rebuild their numbers, musk oxen had come 'perilously close' to joining the hairy mammoth and the dodo."

A bull musk ox

Chapter Five

Qiviut

"Odd name, musk ox," mused John who had been listening attentively. "I think of an ox as a castrated male of the bovine species. Yet you have a heifer and call her 'musk ox.'"

Clarence absently stirred his second cup of coffee before replying. "Early explorers labelled musk oxen a variety of things: a sort of ox, a type of buffalo, a northern hairy sheep, a goat-antelope. They were all wrong. Even the name, musk ox (ovibos moschatus) which means musky sheep-cow is misleading."

The conversation continued as Clarence shared much of what he'd learned over many years of reading and research. "The musk ox is a specie whose nearest living relative is thought to be the takin, a thick-set, cumbersome appearing native of eastern Tibet.

"Dr. Paul Moody, through scientific study of musk ox blood believes they bear about the same relationship to goats as bison do to cattle. Dr. John Teal, considered a world authority on musk oxen, says their behavior reminds him of goats."

"Where does the prefix "musk" come from?" John wanted to know. "I couldn't detect any odour at all when we unloaded the heifer."

"Musk oxen don't have a musky smell. They don't even have the gland to produce musk, so how they earned the misnomer of 'musk ox' is a mystery.

"Some people suspect it was because of the pungent odour of their droppings on the wet tundra. Others suggest that it might be connected to the smell bulls give off during the rut. I wonder if sixteenth-century explorers didn't purposely add the word 'musk' to their name hoping to profit from it financially?"

In response to John's terse "How so?" Clarence continued.

"Perhaps money-hungry adventurers hoped the word "musk" would spark interest, stimulate financial support for future expeditions to the north.

"Remember, this was at a time when musk was the essential base for the world's finest perfumes. It was also when personal cleanliness was considered a somewhat nebulous virtue even among the very wealthy, and when all manner of household filth was customarily dumped from windows to turn gutters into open sewers. So naturally perfumes, with their ability to camouflage a great variety of stenches, were in high demand. So why wouldn't the word 'musk' trigger expeditions to far away lands?"

As I took another pan of cinnamon buns from the oven my mind sifted through other things I had heard about musk oxen.

Although musk oxen have been erroneously named, they do have some similarity to sheep and cows. They are cloven-hoofed ruminants with four teats, beef-like meat, and wool recognized as the finest in the world. Both sexes have massive, permanent horns. The cow's milk is rich and tasty according to those few people who have tasted it.

Bulls in the Arctic have been shot weighing as much as 900 pounds, whereas animals captured as calves and fed a nutritious southern diet have reached weights of 1,400 pounds. This indicates musk oxen grow considerably larger under ideal food conditions. Given the added advantage of selective breeding, musk oxen might conceivably compare some day in size to cattle

On permafrost ranges musk oxen feed on whatever

grasses, sedges, and woody growth is available. In more southern areas they eat a lot of browse, often using their shoulder and front feet to push over two-inch diameter saplings to get at the more succulent branches and leaves.

Musk oxen customarily feed for approximately two hours, then rest for two hours, breaking their day into series of eat-sleep periods.

Because of the difference in their diets musk oxen and caribou can co-exist on the same range. However, unlike caribou, musk oxen are not migratory. In summer they do move about a lot, rarely staying more than a day in any one spot, but in winter they feed in one place for several days. This might be because travelling is difficult, but more likely it is their way of conserving heat and energy.

The hooves of the musk ox are wide with deep concave inner surfaces and a sharp horny outer rim that enables animals to move safely over hard snow. A softer, broad heel, similar to a horse's frog, gives them traction on rock. The hooves are not covered in qiviut. However considerable hair does sprout from between the clefts.

"Bearded One"

The coat of the musk ox is a two layer affair. The long outer hair looks coarse and has been compared to a Hawaiian dancer's grass skirt. It sways close to the ground giving the impression the animal, when seen from a distance, is a near shapeless blob, with only the massive horns indicating which end is front.

The outer hair, guard hair as it is often called, is, in spite of its coarse appearance, surprisingly soft to the touch. It grows to an amazing length. Up to nineteen - inches on the flank and twenty-five inches on the throat. No wonder the Eskimo people give the animal the picturesque name "Oomingmak" which means "Bearded One"

The dense under-layer of fine wool known as qiviut covers the entire animal except for his horns, hooves, lips, eyes and a small patch on the tip of his nose. To the musk ox this coat means 'life'. Without it they couldn't live in a land of constant bone-chilling cold, cold driven in and compounded by the raging blizzards routinely sweeping across the top of the world.

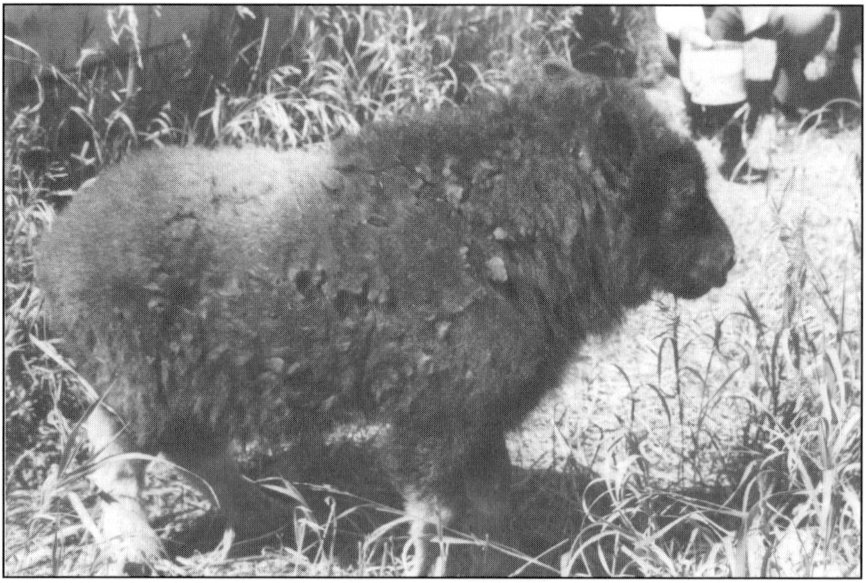

Musk ox shedding

In summer the shedding qiviut hangs from the animals in untidy streamers giving them a ragged, moth-eaten appearance. Sometimes called the Golden Fleece of the Arctic, qiviut, if available in commercial quantities, would have exciting potential.

Textile experts feel confident that if blended with synthetics, qiviut would make a type of vicuna cloth that would revolutionize the world of fine fashions.

As early as 1917 Vilhjalmur Stefánsson, impressed with the meat and wool of the musk oxen, foresaw their potential, and pressed for their domestication. Other men of vision agreed.

But nothing was done about it. Musk oxen remained shrouded in mystery until interest in them was revived about the middle of the twentieth century. Then thirty-four musk ox calves were caught in Greenland and taken to the University of Alaska at College on the outskirts of Fairbanks, where it was hoped they could be established on a commercial basis.

However, this venture wasn't the success that had been hoped for. Alaskan grizzlies got blamed for making the calves so unmanageable they chased people up trees. It was finally decided to release them on Nunivak Island, a tiny island in the Bering Sea where there were no wolves or grizzlies to harass them.

Although that venture failed, interest in musk oxen smoldered. In 1954 John Teal, spurred by Stefánsson's enthusiasm, got permission from the Canadian Government to capture musk ox calves on the strict understanding no adults were to be harmed.

Teal made two capture expeditions to the Thelon Game Reserve. The first, in 1954, succeeded in capturing three calves, which were taken to Teal's farm in Vermont, U.S.A. The following year four more calves were taken and added to the original three to become the world's first "domestic" herd of musk oxen.

Unfortunately the Vermont project was not the success Teal hoped for. Cows either did not conceive, or if they did, the resulting calves often died. Perhaps the hot, damp climate was unsuited to an animal used to the dry, hard cold of the North.

In 1964 an effort was made to establish a herd in a more congenial atmosphere. Teal, in collaboration with the University of Alaska, the Institute of Northern Agricultural Research, and supported financially by the W.K. Kellog Foundation, organized two more expeditions to capture musk-ox calves.

This time the capture was made from the exploding musk-ox population on Nunivak Island where the original thirty-three animals had increased to nearly seven-hundred and fifty. In the years 1964 and 1965 ten males and twenty-four females were caught. These were taken to the College Research Institution on the outskirts of Fairbanks.

It was some of those calves, grown into great lumbering cows, we met on our first visit to Alaska. And now we had a musk-ox calf of our own.

Chapter Six

How Musk Oxen Herds Began

We had hoped to find Musky quieter when we returned to the barn. Instead there was more fresh blood dripping from above one eye. The scraggly white hairs on her forehead were matted with gore. She was still trying to bash her way to freedom.

I gulped, remembering a bull at Fairbanks. He had picked a fight with a rival and came out of it with a cracked skull.

"Clarence" I urged, "We've got to do something. Do you think a drink of water might help?"

He looked glumly at the remains of the battered pail. "I suppose it wouldn't hurt to try again."

I trotted off to get another pail.

My husband took it from me and carried it to Musky's pen. The next moment something shot by me like a rocket, narrowly missed Clarence's head, splashed water onto our clothes. Water that froze almost instantly, festooning us in icy scrolls.

My husband tossed the remains of that pail alongside the other. "Maybe we should try snow." There was an under-layer of doubt in his voice as he kicked loose a good-sized chunk from a crusted drift near the door and held it above Musky's head.

She looked at it, eyes wild, hackles high, but to our surprise she didn't lunge at it. Instead her expression gradually changed from one of hostility to cautious interest.

In another moment she was reaching up, biting off greedy chunks of snow.

We watched in fascination as she ate the first lump, then a second and a third. The fourth got a different reception. She snorted and tried to ram it, which perhaps was her way of saying “I’ve had enough.”

Anyway we breathed a little easier now. A dehydrated animal will die faster than a hungry one .

Realizing our heifer would have many changes to adjust to, and wanting to make it as easy for her as possible, Clarence had brought home a bag of the musk-ox pellets she had been eating at the zoo. They were a scientifically mixed ration, everything a musk ox needed to stay healthy. He even brought along her feed dish.

But now when she saw it in front of her, half full of pellets, it seemed as alien to her as the water buckets. It got the same reception. Pellets fell around us like hail. Some landed in her pen. We hoped she would eat them during the night.

There is something about the quiet hush of night that soothes and comforts nature’s frightened creatures. Perhaps it would be so with Musky.

* * *

It seemed like the middle of the night when Clarence crawled out of bed and began pulling on his clothes. There was no need to ask what he was up to. He was going to check on Musky.

We had gambled that a six-month-old calf would be young enough to adjust to capture. And a new home. After yesterday we weren’t sure.

“Too bad we couldn’t get a two-week old animal,” I muttered as I sat up in bed and pummelled my pillow. “Then it would imprint and think we were family.”

“Imprint!” Clarence scowled impatiently and stalked out of the room.

"Well, what's so unusual about that? " I muttered as he left. On the ranch we often see temporary imprinting. Although we may not call it that.

A very young calf will sometimes get confused or frightened and run away from both the herd and its mother. When it does, trying to bring it back is like trying to haze a skittish mouse. However I've found a way that sometimes works.

If I gallop my horse alongside the runaway calf it starts thinking the big animal running beside it must be its mother and crowds close to the horse. Then it's easy to bring the calf back to the herd. But it's not always easy to get the calf "unstuck" from the horse. It may take minutes before the bellowing, harried dam can convince her offspring that she, not the horse, is the rightful mother.

I sighed. Musky was too old for imprinting.

Suddenly I realized I was cold, the bed no longer felt warm and cozy. Wrapping a house-coat tightly around me, and sticking my feet into chilly slippers, I wandered aimlessly around the house, peering often through frosty windows trying to pierce the blackness of an early winter morning. Nothing. Only stars shimmering cold and impersonal, blinking at the world from a million light years away. What was taking Clarence so long?

Should I get dressed and go see? Or wait? I pulled the house-coat tighter and shivered.

Then familiar footsteps crunching through the snow and I was at the door asking anxiously of the darkness, "How is she?" yet dreading the answer.

The cloud of cold air that burst into the room with Clarence couldn't blot out the haggard lines around his eyes.

"She hasn't touched her food," he said as if that should tell me all I needed to know.

"But how is she?" I insisted. "What is she doing?"

"She's still charging," he said in his slow, quiet way, "but not so wildly. Maybe she's settling down some. Or maybe she's just exhausted."

Then voices called down from upstairs. "Happy Anniversary Mum and Daddy." We looked at each other a little sheepishly. It was December 30th, 1971. And we had forgotten.

"How about that?" I teased. "Married twenty-five years and playing second-fiddle to a musk ox." He grinned and gave me a hug.

Anniversary or not there were things to be done. Musky had to have a shot of Pen Strep, an antibiotic to help prevent pneumonia.

The first question was "How large a dose?"

Clarence phoned the vet in Wainwright. He didn't know as much about musk oxen as we did, but he thought it would be safe to give her 5 c.c. . . . the same dose as one would give a calf.

The second and bigger question was how does one go about giving a hypodermic injection to an animal as wild and unmanageable as our musk ox?

"Don't worry Mum." Heather tried to comfort me. "Daddy will figure out a way."

I knew he would. But I was glad John was here to help. The girls and Rod too. They were all good around animals. Even Grandpa. At 85 he was sure to have some good ideas."

After breakfast the men rigged up a temporary squeeze using a gate already in the barn. It had been built to swing and crowd a musk ox out of the larger area and back into the training pen. A few alterations and it became one side of the squeeze. The barn wall became the other. The squeeze was then heavily padded with foam. We didn't want her to hurt herself.

Finally everything was ready. The hypodermic syringe

was filled with just the right dose. Clarence, Rod and John were positioned where they could open and close gates with split-second precision, because timing would be vital. The girls and I were prepared to help in any way we could if things went wrong. Grandpa held the syringe.

When Rod lifted the latch on the training-pen door allowing it to swing partially open everyone tensed. We expected Musky to charge through it and be in the squeeze before she realized her wild dash hadn't been to freedom after all. But Musky didn't move.

Rod reached out and pushed the door wide open. She watched suspiciously.

He waved a mittened hand above her head. Nothing happened. He waved again, this time closer. She snorted, jumped up and came back down exactly where she had started. We hadn't expected this.

Musky wasn't about to risk exchanging the place she had grown accustomed to for the unknown. She preferred the security of knowing there was a wall behind her. In the Arctic when a lone musk ox senses danger, it backs up against a rock or a cliff. Or anything that will offer protection for its hind quarters, leaving its head free to slash and hook at the enemy.

Rod kept baiting Musky with his hand until she finally charged, stamping from the pen and into the squeeze on a burst of fury. When she did John quickly closed the gate behind her, shutting off her hope of backing out.

Twisting and writhing she threw herself furiously against the confining planks. When they didn't so much as shudder she gave up and stood with heaving sides. Her head drooped like a wilted flower until it almost touched the floor. But there didn't seem to be anything wrong with her so Clarence felt for a well-muscled spot and injected the Pen-Strep. She didn't flinch. Or show any sign she had felt the needle.

Musky looked so quiet I reached out to pat her. That was a mistake. It was as if I had flipped a switch that released a violent surge of unadulterated fury. "Crack Pot!" I exploded as I backed off in amazement "Doesn't flinch at a hypodermic injection. Then goes berserk when a hand barely touches her."

I watched the men trying to get Musky out of the chute and back into her pen, wondering if we would ever really understand what makes a musk ox tick.

It was senseless to try to push her backwards. Even a light touch on the shoulder or rump made her give an explosive snort and plow ahead, bashing her head into the padded front of the squeeze. There was fresh blood on it now.

Then without any warning she shot backwards like a stone from a slingshot and came to a jolting stop with her rump rammed tight against the end of the training pen. Someone shut the door.

Clarence mouth twitched into a tiny grin. But there was a troubled look in his blue-green eyes as he reached for his mitts.

Later that day I tried to coax Musky to eat by holding a wisp of alfalfa hay above her. The way Clarence had done with the snow. She showed no interest. I dangled it closer. That triggered charges so abusive even the air seemed to be holding its breath.

Well, if Musky chose not to eat there wasn't much we could do about it. Nor were we surprised.

We'd had similar experiences with horses. Some animals will go off their feed for a day or two when first brought into the stable after a few weeks on pasture. Terry Lee's show mare, Gango Firefly, often refuses to drink water when away from home. However we discovered a partial solution to this. She likes milk.

If Arabian horses, after thousands of years of domestication, still pull tricks like that, why shouldn't a musk ox?

Never-the-less I was worried about Musky. So I spent most of the afternoon trying to make her understand I wanted to be a friend. Animals, like humans, need a friend.

Suddenly the dog started barking. I heard car doors slam.

Good Grief! I'd forgotten. Again. This was our wedding anniversary. Folks were coming to help us celebrate it.

And here I was, in a heavy parka smelling of barn and animals, pants with a patch on one knee, an old cap jammed down over my ears, chore boots on my feet and mitts with darns in the liners. Frost clung to my eyelashes. I knew my nose must be red. It was tingling from cold and dripping like a leaky faucet. Oh Damn! Where was that kleenex?.

"Don't worry," Clarence who had just come in, comforted me. "You look good to me, and they won't notice."

He was right.

Our visitors streamed towards us calling excitedly. "Is the musk ox in there? Can we see her?"

"Only a quick peek. She's very nervous."

No one was permitted more than a brief look at Musky but it was long enough for her to impress them.

One awe-struck youngster crept close to his mother whispering "Is it some sort of dragon Mummy? Does it eat people?" and before she could reply he begged. "Let's go. I'm scared."

"Think you'll ever tame her?" a friend asked Clarence skeptically.

And he, with a slow, almost shy smile, had to admit she was pretty fierce.

* * *

Four months earlier we had been at the Musk Ox Farm at Fairbanks the day their calves were separated from their mothers and put two to a pen for weaning. When all the calves were paired, the manager, Dee McConnell, went into the pens and fastened a two-inch wide leather strap around each animal's neck.

This was the first time those calves had been handled. Yet none of them made any attempt to attack him. Most were restless. A few tried to run (in a two-by-six pen there isn't much room for running) but for the most part they seemed to consider it was of no great importance that a strap was being buckled around their neck.

When that was done McConnell poured milk supplement into a quart-size jam can fitted with a sheep nipple. He made sure the lid was on tight before handing it to his helper. Then he straddled a calf, gripping it with his knees in a teach-a-calf-to-drink stance, his hands on either side of the leather collar. While he held the animal steady his helper shoved the nipple into the calf's mouth.

At first the calves tried to jerk their heads away so the jam can got a few bumps. Bumps that had no similarity at all to the murderous way Musky went for things she didn't like.

A few calves accepted the nipple as eagerly as if it was their mother's teat. Others tried to shake off their "rider" or stamp on his toes. Some clamped their mouth and obstinately refused all attempts to push a teat into it. Most were sucking greedily within a day or two.

Hand-feeding newly-weaned calves is routine at Fairbanks. Through it McConnell hopes to establish a bond between himself and the calf similar to a mother-offspring relationship. If by using a nipple and milk-replacer he can duplicate that feeling of security, the calves soon learn to trust him. And once they do, they become very easy to handle.

It sounded logical. And it looked easy.

We came home convinced musk ox calves don't fight as much as same-age Hereford range calves would have done under similar circumstances.

Something else at the Fairbanks musk-ox farm impressed us. Having gone there with reports of the wild, cantankerous nature of musk oxen firmly stamped on my mind, I wasn't prepared for what I saw.

On our arrival at the farm Dee McConnell asked if we'd like to walk with him out to the musk ox pasture. Of course Clarence said yes. We hadn't gone far when a great shaggy beast left the herd and started towards us. Two more followed in a purposeful fashion. I looked around uneasily. The gate seemed miles away. There was no place to hide. Nothing to climb. We might as well have been on a vast desert where the horizon drifts into the sky.

My husband and McConnell kept right on walking and talking. They didn't even LOOK concerned. Nervously I edged in behind them.

The musk oxen with dirty white blotches on their foreheads and saddles, looked like cumbersome brown bears after a recent raid on a flour barrel. They tramped steadily closer, their long skirts almost brushing the ground.

My breath began making queer sucking sounds, like pulling bare feet out of Grande Prairie mud. Icy fingers raked my spine.

The air felt suffocating and tense. I wanted to run. Instead I tried to stifle the fear cluttering my throat as the first of the three musk-ox cows planted herself squarely in front of Clarence and began smelling his hands and coat, but especially his pockets.

Good Grief! She was looking for treats.

Having brought no goodies Clarence scratched heads instead, which seemed to the animals' liking for they sidled closer.

I inched nearer and was soon scratching and petting too. "Gee. They're tame. Were they orphans you bottle-fed as calves?"

Before McConnell had time to answer Clarence asked. "How many generations since these were wild?"

McConnell's smile wrinkled his face as if it were a crumpled brown paper bag.

"Those," indicating the pair that at that moment were examining my pockets, "are two of the original calves captured six years ago on Nunivak Island. They probably never saw a human until the day they were caught. Yet within weeks they were following us like dogs."

We had long talks with Mr. McConnell and his staff about musk oxen. We watched two men, one on a motor scooter, the other on foot, bring in a herd of thirty musk oxen. As soon as the animals saw the scooter approaching they started bunching up, then scampered bucking and frisking into the holding pen near the barn.

Afterwards the men remarked the musk oxen had seldom come in with so little trouble. Perhaps the cold drizzle, a prelude to an early September snow, made them easier to drive.

Motor scooters were the farm's "cow ponies." They are OK for herding she-stock and immature bulls, but the riders have big problems outmaneuvering breeding bulls.

Males became extremely dangerous during the rut. They'll attack anything that moves.

A wrecked motor scooter, blitzed just prior to our visit by an ordinarily gentle bull, attested to the truth of this statement. Fortunately the rider was able to jump clear, so he got out of that mishap with only a few scratches. In Norway there is a report of a bull killing a man. Others have had serious injury. Workers at the Alberta Game Farm tell of a musk ox who challenged a half-ton truck and came out the victor. The vehicle had to be hauled away as junk.

Mr. McConnell let us watch yearling heifers being put through a scales and their weights recorded.

They weren't herded as we drive cattle, but rather a man stood at the front of the scales and coaxed each animal in with a willow branch or the promise of grain.

Some of the animals were reluctant about getting weighed and hung back, crowding to the far end of the holding pen. Instead of getting in with them and Hi-yi-ya-ing them down the chute and onto the scales as we would have done with cattle, the men left them alone and went to another job. Later in the day when the men returned to finish the weighing the animals were easily tempted onto the scales.

This method of handling musk oxen, so different from how we manage ranch stock, interested us.

We asked what would happen had the men tried to force the musk ox onto the scales. We didn't get a definite answer, but were left with the impression it was better to lead a musk ox than to attempt to drive it. And that is a theory, that after having had some experience with musk oxen, we came to agree with.

While at the musk-ox farm we watched a fight between a pair of immature bulls. They went at it with vim and determination. First backing off to snort and stamp then hurtling together, hairy avalanches of destruction crashing head against head with a crack that resounded like an exploding cannon. Then they'd back away, cold eyes glittering with intent fixed on those of their opponent. While reversing they'd shake their massive heads slowly from side to side as if saying "Ouch! That hurt!"

But don't get the idea they were giving up. They were only backing for another charge. And this goes on until one animal decides he's had enough and wanders off. When mature dehorned bulls fight they sometimes crack their skulls, so powerful is their charge.

In spite of knowing bulls are dangerous and must be treated with respect we had come away from our visit to the musk-ox farm in Alaska confident we would have no problems handling musk oxen. With a training pen built to Fairbanks specification there seemed no reason to anticipate trouble in duplicating their taming methods. Smug with ignorance we told ourselves "those who think musk oxen are cantankerous are out to lunch."

That was before Musky arrived. She lost no time letting us know we were the ones "out to lunch."

Musky was two months older than the calves we'd watched at Fairbanks. She was of the Ovibos m. moschatus strain found in the Thelon Game Reserve, whereas the Alaskan herd had come originally from Greenland, home of the smaller Ovibos m. wardi strain. But was that enough to make such a difference in her behavior? We didn't know.

Yet it wasn't hard to understand her fear of us. Not when one remembered that for centuries her ancestors had been driven further and further north by ruthless humans who wiped out entire herds in the bloody name of sport. Only the wildest, most wary animals survived to pass on the genetic traits that had saved them . . . traits that were compounded and intensified over the years, until it was a part of Musky's heredity to fear and hate humans.

Taming her would be no instant, ready-mix affair. It would take patience, understanding and lots of time.

Chapter Seven

Musky Tries Carrots and Sugar

The next morning, Musky, having drunk water during the night without wrecking the pail, was given more space. She could now go out into an area twice the size of a large dining-room table. Here, with pellets in a feed-box and alfalfa hay beside it, we hoped she would feel more at ease.

However, trips to the barn always found her backed defensively into the far corner, head down and ready to charge. If we moved she snorted and stamped, but if we stood perfectly still her main concern seemed to be rubbing an itchy spot below her eye on an extended foreleg. But her eyes, smoldering and darkly defiant, watched every move we made.

Nothing escapes a musk-ox eye. They protrude from the side of the head allowing the animal good backwards as well as forward and sideways vision. When alarmed or under duress they bug out still further.

Their eyes adjust to a wide range of light intensities, varying from months of almost complete darkness to periods of intense glare. In scientific jargon the pupil of the musk-ox eye is horizontally rectangular with corpora negra present along the pupil margin, which basically means their eyes have a split pupil arrangement that permits complete closure under intense light, while many large sensory rods give the animal good night vision.

When Musky blinks her lids roll from both top and bottom to meet at the horizontal center of her eye. This chicken-like flipping of membranes gives one the impression it's a clownish wink. Actually there's nothing doltish about it, but a very practical arrangement that shields the eye from the dazzling glare of sunshine coming either from above or reflected upward from the snow.

Musky had gone two days without eating enough to notice. She must be hungry.

I hoped to coax her into starting to eat by offering her some of the longest, greenest alfalfa hay I could find. It was so long it came within inches of her nose. Is she would stretch her neck, or even lean a little, she could reach it.

Instead she snorted and stamped. Then looking fierce and volatile she went back to rubbing her face.

When a musk ox stamps it half rears, coming down hard on its front feet as if intending to drive them into the ground. (No matter how often I hear it there is something about a musk-ox stamp that never fails to start my tiny body hairs crackling with fright.) And when an animal charges at a punishing stiff-legged punching-holes-in-the-ground stride its best to have sudden and urgent business elsewhere.

However, when Musky didn't follow up her stamp with a charge, I tried again. By jamming my shoulder tight against the planks, I was able to shove the hay almost within reach of her mouth.

This time she gave no warning but flew at me like a mad hornet. I jerked my arm back, then looked almost lovingly at the heavy planks that had saved me.

The next day I offered Musky a carrot. She watched it suspiciously for a long time, blinking her queer eye-dividing blink and rubbing her nose. My patience exhausted I was about to leave when she started towards me, slowly but deliberately.

I watched half expecting her to make a sudden lunge at the carrot. Or at me. When she could reach the carrot by stretching her neck she took it gently from my hand. However, it wasn't until her rump was against the wall she felt safe enough to eat it. With that carrot gone she smacked her lips, came for a second and backed away again,

Yippee! Now I'd finally found something she liked I expected she'd soon be as friendly as the Fairbanks musk oxen. I took a third carrot from my pocket and offered it to her. That one got an entirely different reception. There was a wild mad glint in her eyes as she stamped three times, punctuating each stamp with a menacing snort. It wasn't hard to get the message.

That evening we were surprised, and pleased too, when Delbert Degenhardt, Terry Lee's visiting University class-mate, came in to say with a touch of bravado, "Musky ate two sugar lumps out of my hand. Then she licked it. She acted real friendly."

We loaded him down with more sugar and piled out the door after him. That was another mistake.

Perhaps Musky resented an audience, or perhaps like the carrots, two sugar lumps were enough. Whatever the reason she stood in the corner snorting and stamping, the cold hard glitter in her eyes denying she had ever made a friendly overture to anyone.

Chapter Eight

Friendship with Gango Brandy the Colt

As a family we had given up Christmas holidays to build a corral suitable for a musk oxen. Now Clarence decided it was time to make use of it. On New Year's Day Musky was allowed out into the corral for the first time.

She had watched Clarence open the barn door, fasten it so it couldn't blow shut, then walk way. She finally moved towards it as if expecting the door to suddenly slam in her face. When it didn't she stood in the open doorway a long time cautiously looking around.

With head high and nostrils dilated she sniffed the breezes for possible trouble. Obviously she didn't intend to be caught unawares.

Eventually she inched ahead and put one foot down into the snow. But almost immediately she lifted it, shaking it as if needing to convince herself nothing had happened, then put it down again. A second foot soon followed the first. She inspected it as she had the other.

After that it wasn't long until she stepped out and walked carefully to the middle of the corral.

When she saw us watching her she whirled, head down and on the defensive. But she didn't move. Not until Rod walked to the opposite side of the corral. Then, perhaps because she felt uncomfortable about having "enemies" on two sides, she snorted and galloped stiff-legged back into the barn.

Clarence grinned at me. "See. You needn't have worried I'd have trouble getting her into the barn at night."

As soon as we left, Musky came out into the corral again and began nosing half-heartedly at the underbrush.

Later in the day when a blizzard blew in she became restless, galloping about, head high, long hair streaming behind her . . . a wild, restive creature longing to be free. She began a careful inspection of the corral, sniffing it and giving it the odd experimental bunt.

Sometimes she reared and stood with her front feet high on the planks, looking to see if there was any way to get over the top. We were glad we had taken the precaution of building the bottom three feet of fence solid, with no toe-holds.

Musky was fidgety for the rest of the day as if her instincts were relentlessly driving her. Perhaps the wind brought with it nostalgic longings for the cold and barren Arctic, and tundra ranges were calling her to come.

Actually Musky seemed to benefit from the storm. It did something for her appetite. That evening she began nibbling pellets. We hoped she would soon be eating enthusiastically.

Instead, the next day we had another cause for concern. Clarence came in at noon to say Musky seemed uneasy, lying down, then getting up again almost immediately. Such behavior in a horse would be almost a sure sign the animal was in a lot of pain from colic. And we'd know how to handle it. But what does one do for a colicy critter as wild and unpredictable as Musky?

We worried about it throughout the noon meal, discussing possible plans, then quickly rejecting them as unworkable. Fortunately Musky herself saved us from having to take any decisive action, for when we looked at her again she seemed content and quite at ease.

That started us wondering if she had been in distress. Or if she had only been trying to work snow into her thick coat for an Arctic style dry-cleaning. Like a chicken's dust bath. A cow pawing dirt over her back. Or a horse rolling.

With the Christmas holidays over we soon got into a regular routine with Musky.

She was out in the corral during the days now, but shut in the barn at night. Not because she needed the shelter but because Clarence wanted to get her used to going in for extra food.

Even though she never seemed anxious to eat either pellets or alfalfa, she did like beet concentrate well enough to spend considerable time picking it out from among the other pellets in her feed box. But she didn't consider it special enough to warrant going into the barn to get it. Unless she was in the right mood. Which wasn't often.

It hadn't taken Musky long to learn she was to go into the barn when Clarence called "Musky Get!" She'd run in snorting and stamping as soon as she saw him coming and then wait for him to swing shut the gate that stopped her from running out again. But now that began to change.

Sometimes she'd snort defiance and run in a high bounding gallop to the opposite side of the corral where she'd stand stamping like a naughty child. When Clarence walked to that side, repeating "Musky Get!" she'd run back to the other side. At first when that happened all it took to get her to go into the barn was for Rod or I to stand across from Clarence. But that didn't work for long either.

There were days when she'd gallop stiff legged around and around the corral, pounding past the open door as if it was a solid wall. Then when she'd finally fling herself angrily into the barn she'd come flouncing out again before anyone could get to the door and shut it. Then the business of trying to get her in had to start all over again.

It was a game for Musky. She liked it because she always won. There was no way anyone could get to the door fast enough to shut it before she came shooting out again.

Clarence couldn't let a musk ox outsmart him so he rigged up an ingenious device of strings and pulleys so the door could be pulled shut by someone standing outside the corral. That became my job.

(We still didn't risk going into the corral to chase her in so we had to get her into the barn from the safety of the other-side-of-the-fence.)

When Musky found her game spoiled, she thwarted us by not going into the barn at all. Now when Clarence shouted and waved his arms at her she either ignored him with bored indifference or looked as if she was wondering why 'silly humans' indulge in such extravagant contortions. My husband would have to think of some other way to get her into the barn.

He got four empty five-gallon tin grease pails from the shop and lined them up outside the musk ox corral where they would be within easy reach.

When it was time for Musky to go into the barn he heaved the first pail over the fence and as it rolled clattering and clanging towards her he yelled "Musky! Get!"

Musky got. The instant the pail hit the ground to hiccup its way crazily towards her she was off and snorting in a head-up ground jarring yo-yo of a gallop that bounced her across the corral and into the barn. I yanked on the twine and the door slammed shut. Another quick pull on a second string swung the gate in the barn into place so she was securely fastened in her own pen. It was safe now to go in and feed her.

The pail method was to remain in use for a long time. It seemed a sure and safe way to get Musky into the barn when she was in a perverse mood. But there would come a time when even that didn't work.

Musky still wasn't eating as we felt she should and never showed any interest in food when we were near. Instead she'd watch us suspiciously from the far corner of her pen, while systematically rubbing her face on an extended foreleg.

We were concerned about Musky's finicky appetite and kept wondering what new foods we could tempt her with.

One morning while peeling carrots for dinner I did a few extra and handed them to Clarence. Musky had come for carrots once. Perhaps she would again.

They looked so crisp and tempting that while waiting to see if she'd come for them Clarence bit into one himself, his teeth crunching its succulent flesh. Musky's ears perked, she blinked rapidly and stared. She stopped rubbing her face and took a step towards him. He kept chewing. She took another step. Then another. She was moving at a snail-pace, but she WAS moving.

When she was close enough to reach the carrot by stretching her neck she stopped and took the carrot he was holding out, then carefully backed into the corner to eat it. When it was gone she watched him with a long probing stare but she refused to step up for a second carrot.

"Stupid critter" Clarence muttered to himself. "I'll put you in the training pen and see what you do."

In there Musky couldn't avoid the issue by retreating to a distant corner. So now when a carrot was offered her she snatched at it angrily, grinding it between her teeth and glaring threats out of the corner of her eye.

She ate four more carrots and a cabbage leaf looking as if her rights had been compromised.

Then, with her lips curled into a look of utter loathing, she snatched the fifth carrot, spit it out onto the floor and stamped on it.

She never ate carrots again.

Not long after the carrot episode Clarence came in saying he had seen Musky chewing her cud. That was a good sign.

"And right now," he continued happily "She's frisking in the snow like a puppy chasing its tail."

That I wanted to see. Throwing a coat around my shoulders I stepped outside. Sure enough, she was frolicking and bucking, jumping in and out of snow-drifts like a Florida youngster seeing snow for the first time. When she saw me she bawled. My ego said "She's inviting you to come and join her fun." My common sense replied "Nonsense." But no matter, we were glad to see her in a playful mood.

That evening after putting feed out for Musky, Clarence, concerned that he still wasn't winning her confidence, sat down on a stock-pile of hay in the alley-way of the barn. Instead of rubbing her nose and watching him with her usual suspicion she surprised him by immediately walking towards the hay. He was soon to get an even bigger surprise.

She didn't stop at the feed Clarence had put out for her, but pushed her nose between the planks to sniff his pant-leg. Its smell apparently satisfied her for she stood quietly beside him until he picked up a spear of hay and pretended to eat, making loud chewing sounds. Musky looked at him carefully, then nosed about in her own feed and began to eat, picking up big hungry mouthfulls and chewing them with noisy gusto.

Finding it awkward to sit cross-legged for long, Clarence eased his cramped legs by stretching out full length. As he did Musky came closer and lay down beside him, leaning her shaggy body against the fence as if wanting to get as near to him as possible.

After a while the cold knifing through, despite the

heavy winter clothing, warned him he would soon have to move. However, he waited a few more minutes wondering what effect his leaving would have on Musky. He soon found out.

The instant he started to move she was up and gone, stamping furiously towards the far corner, where she whirled to face him, head down and snorting a fierce denial her brief lapse into friendliness had ever happened.

We couldn't explain her behavior but it made us more certain than ever. Musky needed company.

Clarence, believing she would be immune to diseases that effect horses, said "Tomorrow I'll fix up a little pen alongside her corral. What pony should I put in it?"

Gango Brandy, a ten-month-old, somewhat skittish, high-strung, Arab-Welsh colt was my choice.

The next morning Clarence brought in more corral sections with churchill, our pet name for the front-end loader. Horses, and cattle too, before they become used to seeing it bring them their feed, gallop off in real or pretend fright whenever the big machine comes near them. But Musky showed no fear of churchill, only an insatiable curiosity. She moved along her paddock fence, keeping abreast of it, watching as panel after panel was hoisted up to come down in corral position with a heavy thunk.

Rod watched Musky as she studied every move churchill made. "Looks as if she wants to learn how to run it" the boy remarked dryly.

As soon as the corral was finished I led Brandy into it. He had never been separated from his equine companions. So I expected him to tear around, whinny and kick up quite a ruckus.

Instead, when I slipped off his halter and closed the gate, he turned and walked inquiringly towards Musky. She walked towards him. Neither had seen an animal resembling the other before, yet they unhesitatingly touched noses through the rails. Musky gave a little snort. Brandy shot her a "now whatcha do that for?" look. Then turned and took a mouthful of hay. She watched him for a few minutes, then began eating too.

From then on when Brandy ate, so did Musky. When he left for the horse barn at night her deep guttural bawl seemed to be pleading "Don't leave." And in the morning it said brightly. "Gee, I'm glad you're back." Brandy liked her too but in a condescending sort of way. As if he considered her to be lower caste than a colt who carried Khem's royal blood in his veins.

On a morning so cold the mercury cowered out of sight I discovered we had a colt sick with distemper. None of our horses had had it. It seemed likely it would rage through the entire herd. There could be deaths. I gulped. What about Musky?

We didn't anticipate she would contract an equine malady, but we couldn't be sure. It would be tempting fate to risk keeping an exposed colt next to her, so she lost her companion. But she didn't lose her appetite. It would be a long time before we had any further concerns about her not eating.

Chapter Nine

Musk Oxen and Cattle

Musky was creating a stir in the district. People called to say they heard we had a buffalo, a yak, or a cross between the two. Some came expecting to see an animal the size of a hippopotamus. Others said she reminded them of a bear. Still others, a pig.

Most of them had never seen a musk ox. Those who had, had seen only a shaggy brown shape in the distance that could have passed for a bear, a yak, or even a Highland cow.

Folks came to look and ask questions. Ours was the only musk-ox project of its kind in Canada. Maybe in the world. Most visitors were blatantly skeptical.

Even friends found it hard to understand us. One, more out-spoken than the rest, stood a long time watching Musky sullenly rubbing her face. He chewed thoughtfully on a spear of hay, then spat it out. "Why the hell do you want musk ox? You've cattle enough to keep you busy, some of the finest Arabians in the country, a good farm. . . . Why damn it man! You don't need musk ox."

"Let's just say its because I've got musk oxen in my blood," Clarence said with a grin."

When visitors saw the pony in the corral beside Musky, or later, the empty corral, they asked "Why don't you put a calf in with her for company?"

The answer to that was simple.

We had purposely put her corral well away from the cattle. There were enough risks involved without deliberately exposing her to the possibility of contracting a bovine disease should one develop in our herd.

When musk oxen, shaggy relics of the ice-age, are transplanted south, they are subject to many of the ailments common to cattle. While they usually respond to the same treatment there didn't seem to be any point in taking unnecessary chances.

When neighbors heard what we had paid for our little musk ox, they shook their heads and said in tones that implied they doubted our sanity "But of course you have her insured?"

That made me want to laugh a little. Or later, cry.

I could still picture the startled face at the other end of the wire the day I phoned the Hartford Livestock Insurance Company and asked, "Do you insure musk oxen?"

There was a long, gasping pause and then a voice sounding incredulous. "Insure a WHAT?"

"A musk ox" I repeated.

"That's what I thought you said."

Then dead silence. A silence so long I was starting to get panicky. What if he had a bad heart? Should I try to get help? I had no idea where.

While these thoughts were racing through my mind and finding no answers, a faint stirring eventually came to me over the phone. I heard a voice bewildered and vaguely unbelieving say "God! I have no idea. But leave me your phone number. I'll find out and let you know."

A week later the call came. "Sorry. We don't insure musk oxen."

Well, we hadn't really thought they would.

Later we learned we could have got insurance to cover the animal during the trip home plus thirty days at a cost in our case of $2,000.

But Clarence, even had he known of it in time, wouldn't have taken out insurance. Thirty days wasn't long enough to warrant that sort of money. He'd take his own risk. He didn't intend to pass up a chance to buy a musk ox just because he couldn't insure it. Not after waiting years for the opportunity.

(Later still when Musky no longer needed insurance we learned Lloyds of London do insure musk oxen.)

Cattlemen, intoxicated with the popularity of exotic cattle, thought we must be intending to mate Musky to beef bulls. Others expected we would A.I. her. The answer to both questions was a positive "No."

Scientific studies had already determined cross-breeding didn't have the remotest chance of success. Even if it did we weren't interested. Clarence wanted musk oxen, not some sort of freak.

As for Artificial Insemination, it seemed to me that getting semen from the male might be as inconceivable as knowing when to inseminate the female. I recalled our talks the fall before with the manager of the Musk Ox Farm at Fairbanks.

Their cows breed naturally during the August-September rut but almost nothing is known about their ovulating cycle. It is believed cows have three, possibly four, periods of estrus during the rut. But animals under close observation at the farm showed little outward sign of being in season. Even shaving the cows' rear ends didn't do anything to help scientists determine a reliable, visible way to ascertain heat. But when bulls become progressively more aggressive, herdsmen know the breeding season can't be far off.

Mr. McConnell told us bulls, and cows too, do a lot of charging about as part of their pre-mating routine. He also told us that although he lived where he overlooked a herd of cows and bulls, he had never actually seen a cow being bred. He suspected they mated at night.

We watched a cow at Fairbanks suddenly break away from her companions and hump off across the pasture at a stiff-legged gallop. A bull shot after her grunting angry sow-like barks. Like a fox running from baying hounds the female streaked across the field with the bull in hot pursuit. Finally, panting and puffing the cow stopped.

"Now he'll breed her" I thought, but with the chase over the bull lost interest and both animals began eating.

A few hours later a bull came stalking majestically out of the herd and started following a cow, sniffing her genitals as would one of our domestic bulls. And like a cow not yet in standing heat, she moved away each time he tried to mount. Then he would step up beside her to lick and nuzzle her face before moving back to try again.

Before long they moved out of sight over the crest of a hill. I turned away not knowing if I'd missed seeing copulation by hours or minutes.

McConnell told us calves are born from April to June. Those dropped in April often encounter Arctic temperatures of thirty below zero (Fahrenheit) or more. With a thick coat of underwool and overhair about an inch long, calves seem better able to withstand the cold than a near-freezing rain. New-born calves quickly learn to take shelter under the long skirts of their mothers where they are completely hidden from sight. In a very few days they are able to keep up with the herd.

Calves begin nibbling at vegetation within a few days of birth. Unless weaned they will suckle the cow for twelve months, or longer, with lactation in the Arctic sometimes lasting up to eighteen months. This gives basis for the theory musk-ox cows only breed every other year, and sometimes only every third or fourth season. Some sightings of twins have been reported, but the average cow on the tundra raises one calf every second or third year. Anyway seeing two calves alongside one cow wouldn't necessarily mean they were twins.

Under ranch management, where calves are weaned and handled as cattle, the musk-ox cow is expected to produce a calf every year, sometimes breeding first as a yearling.

In the Arctic where existence is precarious animals take longer to reach sexual maturity. Cows do not breed until four years of age. Bulls not until they are six. To offset this, musk oxen have a life expectancy of up to twenty-five years.

Northern explorers often remarked on the low proportion of calves in the herds they saw, ranging from none up to 18 percent. This is lower than the ratio of young in caribou herds which is calculated to be about 21.6 percent. That of bison calves in Wood Buffalo Park make up to 23 percent of the herd immediately after calving, but falls to 10 percent (or less) by late winter.

The calving factor is closely linked to the condition of the breeding herd at the beginning of rut. Any animal in poor nutritional health, regardless of the specie, is a slow breeder. This is nature's way of protecting the species from total starvation.

We were feeding Musky a well-balanced diet. She appeared to be a fine big healthy animal so there seemed no reason for concern that if bred she wouldn't produce a calf by the time she was two, or three at the most.

Chapter Ten

She Likes Kids

I began taking hay to Musky every day, calling "Come Musky. Come and get it." Without taking her eyes off me she'd sidle over to the broken stump in the middle of the corral and rub her face on it as if doing so had become the one most important thing in her life..

Damn! If she preferred scratching to eating there wasn't much I could do about it. January's nippy temperatures aren't for standing around. So I'd push the hay between the planks and leave. She'd wait until I reached the house before walking over to sniff it.

Why was it when we were near she seemed to have an itch midway between nose and eye that required continual attention?

"What makes her rub her face like that?" I asked Clarence. "Is she lousy? Or has she some sort of allergy? Maybe to people?"

"It's because she's nervous. In musk-ox language she's saying she's frightened and may charge. I can't explain it except to say when excitement or fear activates an anti-orbital gland just below her eye it produces an oily, near odorless secretion that makes her face itchy. So she rubs it on whatever is handy, usually her front leg.

"There are various other theories as to the probable function of this gland. They range from plastering down the hair around the eyes so the animal can see better, to staking out a territory. I feel a lot more scientific study is needed before the real purpose of the gland is understood. For people like us it's enough to know when a musk ox rubs its face, you better watch out."

As the days snow-balled into weeks there were changes in Musky. Sometimes she'd stop rubbing her face and come up to the hay as soon as I turned to leave. At other times without reason or warning she'd charge, hitting the planks in front of me with ground-jarring violence.

Musky was as full of surprises as our Alberta weather.

One day when Clarence took visitors to see her he discovered a sugar lump in his pocket. He held it out calling "Here Musky." He hadn't the faintest notion she would do anything but snort, stamp and back to the far side of the corral to rub her face.

The visitors, a young couple and their small son, seemed to fascinate Musky. Almost immediately she started sauntering towards them with a warm folksy glow on her face. Reaching the fence she planted her feet in trustful anticipation, and took the sugar lump from Clarence's hand as if she had been doing it all her life . . . whereas she had done nothing like it since the Christmas holidays. Clarence's mouth gaped.

Margaret Hains, Oakville, Ont. makes friends with Musky.

To his further surprise she poked her nose between the planks to sniff the visitors' hands. They hadn't expected this. Nor had he.

The little boy laughed and before he could be warned not to, he had stuck his arm through the rails and was petting her face. Good Grief! Had we attempted anything like this she would have flown into a rage and tried to smash our hand. Yet her eyes looked dreamily gentle as she soaked up attention like a friendly spaniel.

It would be hard to convince those folks musk oxen are dangerous.

"Temperamental" Clarence muttered after they left. But it set us wondering. Perhaps Musky had been attracted to the boy because he was smaller than she, so she hadn't seen him as a threat. That might also explain her actions the time Clarence had sat down (and so looked smaller) and she had lain down beside him.

Or had she recognized the boy as a juvenile? Like herself? Sometimes there does seem to be a natural attraction between the young of different species. I remembered a horse show where Terry Lee was showing a mare on halter. She had left me holding the foal. The little fire-ball had jumped and reared continually, indignant at not being allowed to follow his mother. I wondered if I'd have any toes left when the class was over. Then a small girl and her friends came along ooh-ing and aah-ing over the "beautiful little horse." The colt stopped fighting and began to nuzzle the kids clustered around him like flies around a honey-pot. He looked as happy as a politician amid a gaggle of supporters

When the mare finally came trotting back sporting a red ribbon, the foal ignored her and wanted to follow his new friends.

It wasn't long until our theory that children attracted Musky had further evidence to support it.

A bus load of 4-H kids came to the ranch supposedly to see our horses, but first they wanted to see a musk ox. They piled out of the bus and raced towards Musky's corral and completely encircled it. Talking, laughing, pushing, jostling, they were a rowdy bunch . . . enough to startle most animals.

Any unusual sounds normally sent Musky stamping into her barn. But now she watched, apparently fascinated by the kids tumbling noisily from the bus and streaking towards her. Then with the dignity of an imperial duchess she marched around the corral. Stopping often to sniff the hands reaching to pet her.

Shortly after that Clarence began going into Musky's corral as part of her training. The first time he opened the gate and let himself in with her he felt like a student pilot about to solo. He stood with one hand on the top rail, prepared to swing up if she charged. She stood on the far side of the corral, rubbing her face. Neither took their eyes off the other.

At first my husband only walked along the fence, then back to the gate. He was careful not to go in Musky's direction.

In the days that followed some of the panic left her eyes. She seemed to be accepting him in her paddock. So then he started walking towards her. That brought a look of astonishment and fright to her eyes. She'd throw a wild look at him, then run stamping to the opposite side of the corral.

Clarence moved slowly, careful never to make a sudden move that might invite a charge. Before long he felt confident that although she rubbed her nose constantly, and often snorted and stamped, she wouldn't charge. Unless he cornered her. And he wasn't about to do that.

He had little faith in Dr. Paul Wilkinson's belief,

"Musk oxen won't charge unless they can get a run at their target." Musky could charge in three inches of space.

Nor was he about to experiment with Wilkinson's other claim: "If a musk ox charges just hold your hand out. The musk ox will hit it, then back away." Dr. Wilkinson told us he had seen this happen many times. Our experience with Musky had given us a dim view of this theory, but eventually we did come to believe there might be a degree of truth to it. However, unless one is a disciple of Russian roulette my advice is, "stay clear of a charging musk ox."

Chapter Eleven

Idiosyncrasies

It was inevitable that sooner or later Clarence would want to find out how a musk ox reacts to a rope.

One evening when Musky was in the barn he leaned over the rails and dangled the lasso noose in front of her. She watched it as if hypnotized, but made no attempt to avoid it even when Clarence slipped the loop over her head.

This was a totally different reaction to that shown by cattle. Even day-old calves dodge like frightened mice if they see a lasso. They seem to be born with the instinct to duck from a rope and run.

Musky's trance-like calm lasted only until the rope tightened around her neck. Then she exploded like a bale of firecrackers in a lightning strike. But the storm subsided almost as quickly as it had started. Now she'd move forward in response to the slightest tug on the rope. Clarence looked like a man who has just won a million dollar lottery.

The next time her reaction to the lasso was paradoxical.

"Rod!. What's that noise?"

He listened a moment then was up and running. "It's coming from the musk-ox barn. There must be something wrong." He skidded on the newly waxed linoleum as he made the turn between kitchen and porch, snatching his jacket from its peg as he whizzed past.

Before I got my coat on the noise had stopped. I met the men walking towards the house. Clarence, rope in hand, looked stricken.

"What happened?" I demanded.

"When she felt the slack leave the rope she flew into a enraged frenzy. Her head is gory again, her nose bloody, one leg is scratched and she damaged a horn. I'll have to give up trying to teach her to lead."

I nodded in automatic agreement, hooked my hand through his arm and said dryly "There must be worse things in life than having a musk ox who won't lead."

* * *

When it was time to treat Musky for worms Clarence put the medicine in with her grain knowing she'd likely refuse to eat it. There are horses who can't be tricked into eating grain spiked with worm powder. Dogs, cats too, have an uncanny way of detecting medicine, and avoiding it. But this wasn't so with Musky. She licked her feed box as clean as a hospital sink.

That made us wonder if she'd eat milk supplement the same way. She wouldn't drink it when it was mixed with the water in her pail. And when Clarence had tried the Fairbanks can-and-nipple idea she had glowered at the jam can as if it offended her intelligence. A matter she would put to rights . . . and fast . . . if the can didn't disappear on its own.

But now my husband mixed milk supplement with her nightly grain and watched. She sniffed at it with obvious distaste, fastidiously wrinkling her nose as if hoping to rid herself of the lingering smell. Then she stood a while staring at the feed box as if lost in contemplative thought. Almost immediately she brightened. As if a brilliant idea had suddenly come to her.

She began blowing at the feed causing fine particles of supplement to rise and settle on her face and head, grizzling them like a freshly powdered wig. However blowing took too much time and she was in a hurry to eat. So she tried nosing the supplement out of her box. That didn't work as well as she hoped either, so she started eating, systematically spitting out any milk replacer that found its way into her mouth.

The next evening when she saw Clarence mixing up a similar ration her eyes blazed with outrage. Snorting threats like a ready to erupt volcano, she backed up for a charge.

Clarence stared at her a moment, then shrugged and put the supplement away. He didn't want to put her off eating grain altogether. "Queer appetite," he muttered, "eats worm powder as if it were candy, then threatens me for mixing milk supplement with her grain." He shook his head, his brow furrowed in a mixture of disgust and perplexity.

Musky had other idiosyncrasies.

One sunny afternoon in mid-January Clarence shut her out of the barn. If she couldn't go in and out at will during the day, he hoped she might be more co-operative about going in at night.

That evening when he went to put her in she glared at him, then ignoring the open door she snorted and streaked across the corral to hurl herself into the air as if intending to jump the seven foot high fence. Instead she crashed into the planks and fell back. That made her really mad. Her eyes blazed with anger as she stamped off to try again . . . with no better results.

Blaming the fence for her trouble she began charging into the planks. Battering them with a wild mad glint in her eye, a look of stubborn resolution about her.

Clarence yelled at her like a drill sergeant with frayed nerves. Eventually she turned and galloped flouncing and stamping into the barn, whamming the door jam with her head as she went by, following that up by giving the partition a petulant punch in passing . . . just for good measure.

The water pail was her final target. She landed that a crack that sounded like a high-powered rifle shot. The pail came shooting out through the door. One more sale for the hardware man.

"What put Musky in such a vile humour?" I asked.

"It seems hard to believe but it must be because I shut her out of the barn"

"I wouldn't say that's hard to believe" I teased. "How would you feel if you were locked out of your home?"

The next day the barn door was left open. In the evening Musky was already inside and in a much better humour. She came immediately to eat her grain which was unusual when Clarence was standing beside it. Ordinarily she wanted him at what she considered a safe distance when she ate.

That started us wondering how much effect weather has on musk oxen. Yesterday had been sunny and warm for January. Today we had slipped back into north-pole temperature . . . twenty below zero (Fahrenheit) with a wind that drove cold right to your very innards.

Only a few days ago the land was frozen in the grip of an unusually cold wave. Our thermometer stalled and froze at thirty-nine below for five straight days. Some throughout the district registered from forty-five to sixty-below zero.

Cattle, huddled together to absorb what little shared warmth they could, stood hunch-backed and miserable in a compact mass. Their condensed breath turned them into a foggy blur, some almost too cold and stupid to come for the life-giving feed until Clarence drove them to it.

Horses pawing in the pasture were partially obscured by a haze of self-generated steam that clung around them, graying chestnut coats and forming icicles on nostrils.

Before venturing out we bundled up in layer after layer of warm clothing, until like Egyptian mummies we lost both shape and identity. Even so we hurried with the chores so as to rush back to thaw out in the warmth of the kitchen.

While humans complained about the bitter weather and thought of sultry Hawaiian beaches, Musky basked in the snow, happily chewing her cud, the picture of content.

Often she stood as one entranced, head high, nostrils dilated, hungrily drinking in the frigid air. Sometimes she sauntered about sampling the hay we threw her, nipping off crisp poplar twigs, nosing down through the snow for last year's grass. She seemed to be smiling generously at the shivering world around her.

Chapter Twelve

Political Interest

January stayed cold with a rare intensity that made old houses complain with sharp stinging snaps. Big trees that had weathered many a summer storm suddenly exploded, shattering the stillness with shot-gun detonations, frightening the animals standing dejected and chilled in their shelter. Snow birds froze in their hide-aways. Jack rabbits burrowed deep into the snow for warmth.

The world seemed dead and frozen with only the wind alive, slamming and rattling against its skeleton, whistling down valleys, careening across hill-tops, always driving snow relentlessly before it.

Snow-plows worked around the clock to keep highways passable, but few cars ventured on them.

It was on such a night a knock came on our door. Clarence hurried to open it sure someone must be in trouble. I felt a chilling blast of icy air sweep through the porch and into the kitchen.

"Why Cliff! Come in. What bring you out on such a night?"

It was our member of Parliament, Cliff Downey, stamping snow off his hoots as he removed his fur cap and pulled off his heavy over-coat. "Well, I was passing and thought I'd stop and talk to you about musk oxen," he said blowing on his hands.

The men would discuss many aspects of musk oxen, talking well into the night.

"What do you see as the future for musk oxen on our ranches?" Mr. Downey wanted to know.

"Well Cliff, as you know, the appetite for red meat in areas of the world where rice has been king, is growing. As demand increases, eventually ranches with only so much carrying capacity may find it hard to meet that demand. Perhaps musk oxen could offer an alternative to stockmen with already over-stocked ranges"

In response to Cliff's raised eyebrows, Clarence smiled. "I know you're thinking any increased demand for beef and the consequent price rise would be a dilemma every rancher would be glad to face. But just stop and think a minute. Musk oxen not only flourish in areas of Canada totally unsuited to conventional livestock. They could co-exist with cattle, and actually improve our ranges by eating the scrub growth unpalatable to beef herds.

"And there's another thing. You and I both know areas where brush is creeping in, taking over what was once good grazing land. In some districts whole section have grown up to brush. Yet the sandy soil scarcely warrants the expense of controlling it with sprays or machinery."

Cliff was nodding in silent agreement, one finger absently flicking the release button on his pen.

"Most stockman will tell you the same story. Brush control is so expensive sometimes it seems more efficient to reduce cow numbers. Yet a herd of musk oxen, with their preference for browse could do a good clean up job in these areas. However, unlike fallow deer who are selective and must have browse to survive, musk oxen readily adapt to a variety of grasses and weeds."

As Clarence was speaking our M.P. had occasionally jotted something in a notebook. Now he coughed half apologetically as if there might be a scrap of relative information stuck in his throat that he needed to get out. "Haven't I heard that a musk oxen eats only one eighth as much as a cow? Yet it's half the size."

The rancher's eyes narrowed thoughtfully. "Yes, I've heard that too. But I doubt scientific tests have been done to prove it. However even if it is a bit of an exaggeration, extrapolating the number of musk oxen Alberta's seven-million-plus acres of scrub brush could support is exciting." Clarence ran a forefinger thoughtfully over the rim of his coffee cup. "Something else is exciting. Musk oxen produce the finest wool in the world. Yet they can take care of themselves in coyote country. They have another advantage over sheep whose life expectancy is only five or six years. Musk oxen are known to live up to twenty-five years. Even in the harsh conditions of the Arctic."

"But wouldn't fencing be a problem?" Cliff asked with a twinkle. "The cost of enclosing a section with a seven-foot corral like you have would be astronomical."

Clarence grinned back. "Right. Wild musk are going to need strong fences. Because when they run at something they intend to go through it. But don't forget Cliff, a range cow on the prod needs a solid corral to hold her too. And here is something else to consider . . . if you get a fence-jumper do you keep her to raise more fence-jumpers? No. Of course not. You ship her out on the next liner-load. Cattle are born and bred to mind fences and those who don't aren't around long enough to pass on that trait. Don't you think the same thing could be done with musk oxen?

I have hopes," Clarence went on "that eventually a one-wire electric fence can be used to control them."

Cliff looked surprised. "Electric fencing? That doesn't work with sheep and it looks to me as if musk oxen have an even heavier coat."

"Quite so," Clarence agreed, "But musk oxen are insatiably curious. Their way of investigating any strange object is to walk up and sniff it, touch it with their nose,.

. . . which is one of the few areas of their body not covered in qiviut. Incidentally musk oxen are not only curious. They are remarkably intelligent. I'd gamble that once they touch a wire and get a shock, they'll avoid it like the plague.

"Under domestication animals would be selected for desirable qualities. Things like size, wool quality and production, ease of handling. Perhaps even a polled variety if at sometime a calf is dropped without horns.

"Admittedly this will take time. Lots of time. Taming a wild animal is one thing. Domestication is another, and it's not something that will happen overnight. It's going to take years of work and hundreds of animals. You can't do selective breeding without numbers to choose from. But I'd be happy if I could get a permit to capture as few as half-a-dozen calves."

"How would you go about catching them?" Cliff wanted to know.

"There are several ways it has been done in the past. One is to set up a base camp with a small plane to locate the herds which are often widely scattered. Then when musk oxen with young are sighted a helicopter works well to haze them into a lake, forcing them to swim.

"Calves can't keep up with the stronger swimming adults so they lag behind making it easy for men to drop from the helicopter into the water and catch them. Once the calves are roped they can be dragged ashore for loading or they can be fastened into a sling and hoisted up into the chopper from the water.

"There are some who favour a dry-land capture. John Teal claims to have had good results using a helicopter to herd a cow and calf close to a rocky projection. Keeping her there until a man can climb to the rock above and rope the calf is not usually a problem because any solitary animal tries to get its rump protected by a rock or cliff when harassed. As soon as the calf is roped it's easy to frighten off the cow long enough to load the calf into the helicopter."

"Sounds dangerous to me" Cliff ventured. "I've always understood musk oxen are belligerent devils. Personally I wouldn't want to argue with one. Their horns look deadly."

"Yes, those on captures have reported some scarey moments. But Wilkinson, who has been on a number of musk-ox expeditions says more than four-hundred animals have been captured without anyone being seriously hurt. And only one calf died. That doesn't sound too bad does it?

"Dr. Wilkinson suggests that immediately after capture each calf should receive a mild sedative along with an antibiotic to protect it against pneumonia. Those captured in water should be dried; those chased overland doused with cold water. Musk oxen have sweat glands only on their tongue and feet so they can quickly become overheated.

"Both Teal and Wilkinson agree calves are often neither afraid of, nor antagonistic towards men but quickly respond to human contact.

"To illustrate this point Wilkinson likes to tell about an expedition he was on with photographers sent by a well-known magazine to get pictures of the capture.

"When catching musk-ox calves each man's prime concern is to get his hands on a calf as quickly as possible, with no thought of "how's this going to look on camera?" Consequently the photographers were never in the right spot at the right time. They recorded almost nothing on film.

"However, when the capture ended the men discovered they had a surplus bull calf. (It's virtually impossible to visibly determine sex in calves although some northerners will tell you heifers get a dirty stain on their rear ends at about four months of age.) Anyway, it was decided to release the bull and stage a mock capture for the benefit of the photographers.

"Accordingly the calf was carried to the outskirts of the camp and turned loose. But instead of dashing off so the cameras could get some exciting action shots of the re-capture, he followed the man who had carried him and refused to be chased away.

"Finally in near desperation the calf was picked up and taken as close to his mother as they dared and given a vigorous shove. Only then did he seem to hear the cow's frantic bawling and scamper back to her.

"Men who have been on captures say that within twelve hours the newly-caught calves are offered milk from a nipple. Or willow leaves.

"The wilder ones . . . and there is a wide variation in temperament . . . try to eat, escape, stamp, attack their handler, all at the same time. Hanging onto them is like trying to pin down a whirlwind.

"But within two or three days all the calves come running at the sight of a feeding-pan. From then on taming them is easy. According to John Teal, it is usually permanent."

I sat and listened. No matter how often I heard how men who thought they knew more about musk oxen than anyone else in the world said wild-caught calves were easy to tame, I always found myself wondering what we were doing wrong. We weren't having much success with Musky.

"What's the best time of year to take calves? " Cliff asked.

"August is the month I'd like to try for. Black flies and mosquitoes shouldn't be so bad then. Besides most of the calves would be well started, yet still small enough to handle."

"When you mention black flies and mosquitoes are you thinking of men or musk oxen?" Cliff's eyes sparkled.

The corners of Clarence's mouth crinkled into a half smile. "Men. The only place insects can get a meal from a musk ox is around the rim of the eye, and it's not unusual to see them feasting there in a solid mass until the musk ox becomes annoyed and brushes them off.

"Insects aren't enough of a problem for the musk oxen to need a fly-swatter tail. Which may explain why it is short. Another reason might be there is less of it to drain off body heat . . . an important consideration in periods of intense cold when an animal must conserve energy or die."

I refilled the coffee cups then brought a sample of qiviut for Mr. Downey to feel. He exclaimed over its softness and wanted to know more about it.

Terry Lee wearing a toque knitted from qiviut.

"Similar to cashmere only silkier and with longer fibers" we told him. "According to the experts one pound of qiviut spun in a forty-strand thread will give nearly twenty-five miles of yarn.

"And it has other remarkable properties.

"Studies by Alfred Farrer Barker, professor of textile industries at Leeds University in England, on ovibos wool during the nineteen twenties, indicate cloth made from it wears like merino, is softer than cashmere, and it won't shrink.

"Another plus. It's almost free of grease and can be spun by home spinners just as it comes from the musk ox, without either washing or carding. When processed by commercial mills the yield from raw wool is about seventy per cent. The loose guard hairs shed with the qiviut can be easily removed by machines. (In the months to come we were to learn that hand-picking guard hairs out of the qiviut was a problem for some hobby spinners. Others weren't concerned. They left them in, saying they gave the finished garment a pleasing rustic effect.)

"The yarn can be spun into a gossamer-fine thread or a heavier utility worsted for sweaters or mitts. Would you believe making a sweater from a six-ounce ball of yarn? And I don't mean for an infant, but to fit a man . . . . a man bigger than either of you." And I eyed the two nearly six-footers listening to me.

"Six ounces!" Mr. Downey's voice registered near disbelief. "That seems incredible."

Ignoring that remark I went on to tell how Commissioner Stuart Hodgson of the North West Territories had told me he wears his qiviut sweater whenever he goes on winter trips to outlying Arctic settlement because it is light and warm and "it will wear forever . . . well, maybe only a hundred years."

A few years later I could have told Cliff about a shawl

a Winnipeg spinner, Charlotte Shuttleworth, made from Musky's qiviut. It measured twenty-four by sixty-five inches, plus fringe, weighed almost four ounces, could be easily carried in an evening reticule and yet was so fine it would slide through a woman's wedding ring. Incredible? I saw the shawl.

This shawl was made by a lady in Winnipeg and was so fine it could slide through her wedding ring.

Or I could have told him about the toque prized by Rod, a bush pilot now, because it was the only thing warm enough for Arctic winters yet light enough to wear with head-phones. Or about Clarence's mitts which when thrown in with the rest of the wash come out looking new. But for now Mr. Downey would have to be content with second-hand information.

"Qiviut sounds like a Cinderella's dream. How much does each animal produce?"

"Mature animals produce up to six pounds, younger ones less. This may not sound like much, but when compared to the three-to-ten ounces of pashm, the underfleece of the Kashmir goat that gives us cashmere wool, it's a satisfactory harvest."

Mr. Downey nodded, twisting his wedding band thoughtfully. "The longevity of the musk oxen would add up to a helluv a lot of wool in an animal's lifetime. You say their meat is good. Have you tasted it?"

My husband, a man of vision with the drive and energy to flesh it out was speaking slowly now. "No, but I understand its flavour and texture closely resembles beef. Early explorers spoke of it as tender and luscious.

"Studies indicate both the fat and muscle are low in cholesterol, which could make the meat sought after by diet-conscious people around the world. What if the milk, which explorer Stefánsson claimed tastes like milk from a Jersey cow, is also polyunsaturated? Just last year Dr Wilkinson told me milk from a heifer they had milked at Fairbanks had an excellent flavour. But I'm not aware of other than taste tests being done."

"Milking a musk ox. Now that ought to beat wild-cow milking for kicks! And no pun intended," laughed Cliff. "When the rodeo chaps hear about that they'll be pounding down your door."

Clarence's face crinkled into a grin. "Wilkinson told me the only real problem was finding teats in amongst all the long hair. The little animal soon got so she would stand out in the pasture to be milked."

"Well, I'll be darned! I've milked a good many cows in my life but very few of them were that quiet." Cliff's face took on a kind of wistfulness as he remembered as a boy trying to "so-boss" a fidgety cow into standing in one spot long enough to be milked. She'd wait until he had the pail gripped hopefully between his knees, his hands reaching for her teats, then she'd swat him across the face with a smelly tail and step away, leaving him with eyes smarting, face dirty and fingers closing on nothing but air. After a quarter hour of that, bashing her over the rump with the stool began to seem a reasonable alternative to milking.

In answer to Downey's next question about dressing percentage of the carcass, Clarence told him there is a record of one animal who weighed eight-hundred and fifty pounds after being bled and cooled for a day. When cut up his head weighed forty pounds, the hide and hooves eighty-five, the offal one-hundred and seventeen, leaving more than six-hundred pounds of usable meat. Assuming his live weight was nine-hundred pounds his dressing percentage was better than many domestic cattle.

Other records left by explorers tell us fifty-two animals dressed out at an average of two-hundred and thirty-four pounds, while four head averaged three-hundred and seventy-seven pounds of dressed meat. A herd of ten averaged three-hundred and sixty pounds.

In those days it was the practice to shoot entire herds, some of which would be yearlings or younger, so without knowing the live weight, these figures don't mean much. The instances where live-weight was recorded indicate dressing percentage to be 56% or better. But just as with cattle, a lot would depend on the age and condition of the animal butchered.

"Has anything been done to determine their feed conversion?" Cliff knew feed conversion and rate of gain is always important to feedlot operators.

"Not that I know of, but isn't it reasonable to assume an animal who lives in a land frozen up for nearly ten months out of the year must have a fantastic rate of feed conversion. Even deer (where testing has been done), are more efficient meat producers than the cattle stockmen have been upgrading for centuries."

Mr. Downey agreed the future for domestic musk oxen looked interesting. He was fascinated by their potential to thrive where conventional livestock would starve. Perhaps these animals were the solution to Alberta's millions of acres of near worthless brush.

As our member of Parliament pulled on his heavy coat and got ready to go out into the stormy night we felt he was interested in our venture. But he was only one among many. We weren't holding our breath.

Chapter Thirteen

Musky Wants a Sleigh Ride

The end of January brought some improvement in the weather so Terry Lee and two university friends, Keith and Delbert Degenhardt, came down for the week-end.

The boys went immediately to see Musky. They found her on the far side of the corral too preoccupied rubbing her face to do more than follow them with her eyes.

"Heck! She doesn't look dangerous!" They climbed over the fence and sauntered across the paddock. Musky's itch worsened to panic-bordering urgency. Her eyes protruded like wind-filled sails. The boys not understanding her language felt safe. What was there to be scared of?

Delbert, five-foot-ten, was all muscle and sinew. He had been doing track work preparing himself for a dreamed-of capture expedition to the Arctic. Keith had medals in Judo and felt confident he was a match for a musk-ox calf.

Swinging themselves up and over the fence the boys looked back at Musky. She hadn't moved. She hadn't even stopped rubbing her nose. They found it hard to understand why anyone should be scared of such a harmless looking animal.

"Mr.Burpee," Delbert asked when he got back to the house, "is it O.K. if Keith and I go into the training pen with Musky? She seems real quiet now. Even if she bunted us, it wouldn't hurt. She isn't that big."

Terry Lee's eyebrows arched skyward and she shot me a look that said "Won't they be surprised?"

Rod's snort was derisive.

Clarence didn't say much except. "I wouldn't want you to get hurt."

The boys were confident they wouldn't.

So Musky was put into the training pen and Keith and Delbert stood looking at her. She wasn't as big as a St. Bernard dog. She didn't weigh as much as a three-month-old Hereford calf. If she had horns you couldn't see them. How could she be dangerous?

Yet when Delbert reached down to pet her she exploded as if he had touched off a charge of dynamite. He drew back startled.

"Hell! She didn't act like that the last time I was here. She ate sugar out of my hand."

As he spoke Musky whirled and flew at Keith who had been standing at the other end. Snorting and stamping, lunging up at the faces watching her she left no doubt in any ones mind as to her intentions.

"Still want to go in with her?" Rod grinned.

"Boy! Is she fast! I don't see how she does it." Delbert's frown was puzzled. "That pen is barely two-feet wide yet she swaps ends in it like a yo-yo."

"More like forked-lightning," Keith thought. "Probably packs about the same wallop too." He sounded impressed.

They decided now was a good time to help Terry Lee hitch her grey colt to the cutter.

The next day, Image, the young Arab stallion, teamed with Eldorado a reliable chestnut gelding, were giving the "city" folk cutter rides around the ranch.

Runners crunching, bells ringing, harness jingling, twinkling hooves tossing snow pads back at the young people who ducked and laughed, brought the pasturing horses galloping up to stare in wide-eyed interest. Then having seen their fill, they turned as one and raced bucking and cavorting back the way they had come.

The team, with proud crested manes and arched tails, whisked the cutter past long rows of evergreen sagging with hoar-frost. Then back around a poplar bluff and towards Musky's corral.

"Damn!" I muttered. "Why are they going that way? They'll scare Musky."

But Musky wasn't scared. She watched the fast-moving cutter with interest. Her feet danced with excitement. When it whirled past she galloped and frisked about much as the horse herd had done.

Each time Terry Lee swung her team to repeat the circuit the musk ox watched with obvious fascination. Then as the cutter passed she bucked and cavorted.

The team and sleigh obviously held no threats for her, but what was happening to Eldorado? A horse whose calm acceptance of life's idiosyncrasies makes him a steadying influence when breaking colts to harness was behaving like a nincompoop.

His eyes were popping out of his head. His nostrils flared like giant sea shells as he crowded close to Image each time they passed the musk ox. The more he shied, the happier Musky looked. And the higher she bucked.

The colt, the animal one might ordinarily expect to misbehave, trotted on totally unconcerned about Musky. Except sometimes he gave his team-mate a disgusted look as if saying. "Smarten up dummy. You're crowding me off the trail."

Later over mugs of hot chocolate the young people tossed theories back and forth. Everyone offered possible explanations for Eldorado's behavior. And Musky's. When Rod, munching on a ginger cookie, quipped, "Musky wanted a sleigh ride," Delbert exploded into jeering laughter. But Rod countered with "Well, why not? Teal's Vermont musk oxen liked to climb onto hand-drawn sleighs. As for Eldorado maybe he didn't like Musky's smell."

Which didn't make much sense because Musky had no smell. At least no smell our noses could detect. So what had triggered the geldings warning mechanism? Would we ever know?

Chapter Fourteen

Dehorning Her

Early in February Dr. Leitch from the Wainwright Veterinary Clinic stopped to see Musky. He wanted to make the acquaintance of an animal who would soon become the Clinic's client.

Horns, essential to the survival of wild musk oxen, were believed to be superfluous on the Fairbanks herd. They get broken in confined areas and are dangerous to anything the musk ox took a swipe at. Soon Musky would have to be dehorned. The horn buds were already starting to show.

Perhaps Musky had a premonition of what was in store for her. Maybe she was hoping to throw a scare into the vet that would keep him out of her life forever. Or was it his antiseptic smell that triggered her bad behavior? The day before she had threatened Clarence because his clothes smelled strongly of smoke from having just stoked up the stock-tank heater.

Whatever the cause, when the vet walked into her barn she acted like a caged tornado, lunging into one wall, ricocheting off it, smashing into another. The vet left in a considerable hurry muttering she looked healthy enough to him. He'd be back when the weather moderated.

There is risk in any dehorning but to do it in sub-zero weather is tempting trouble. If frost permeates the open cavity it can cause dangerous complications.

Before the use of caustic-horn pastes became common, dehorning meant immobilizing the cow's head in a squeeze and sawing off the horn. Horns on younger animals were snipped off with a powerful plier-like device known as a dehorner. With either method there was blood. Sometimes only a few drops. Sometimes enough to spray everything within range. Occasionally an animal died from shock.

I dreaded the thought of dehorning Musky. Why couldn't we use caustic paste on her?

I knew the answer before asking the question.

To be effective horn paste must be applied as soon as the bony bud can be felt beneath the skin. In domestic calves this is within a few days of birth. Musk-ox calves are two or three months old before their buds start to develop. Musky at nearly eight months was past the stage when paste could be used.

However Clarence intended to try in on the calves he hoped to raise. Dee McConnell at the Alaska Musk-ox farm thought it might be satisfactory if applied when the horn growth first appeared, but their experiments using radiation to prevent horn growth hadn't been successful. Their best success was with manual dehorning.

He hadn't told Clarence that their Fairbanks Veterinarian had developed a special technique for dehorning musk oxen.

Apart from the dehorning itself, something else was bothering me. How was Clarence going to restrain Musky so she couldn't jerk her head away at the crucial moment.

"Put her in the calf-cradle of course." Clarence's tone implied every farm wife ought to know that.

"How are you going to get her into the cradle? Say 'this way please' then expect her to walk in to oblige you?" My words dripped sarcasm but Clarence replied patiently.

"I'll use the gates Rod and I have been making to form a chute from barn to cradle. When I open the door and chase her out of the barn there'll be no place she can go except down the chute and into the cradle. It'll be easy. You'll see."

I hoped he was right.

* * *

Visitors to our ranch envy what they call our million-dollar-view. They refer to a panorama of rolling parkland that reaches into the distance to culminate twenty miles to the south when it rises to meet the Neutral Hills. Hills so named, legend says, because the mighty Manitou once decreed they must remain forever the neutral ground between two warlike Indian nations. A place where no man's blood must be spilled.

The rolling ranchland of Gango Ranch

Always a kaleidoscope of change the Neutrals become doubly fascinating when an early morning mirage drives them stark and rugged with jutting cliffs and sheer drops, high into the sky. While we watch peaks can form then just as quickly sink into the mists of distance.

In the winter we have a special interest in the Neutrals. When the land is frozen in the deadly grip of winter if there comes a morning when the more distant Nose Hills begin shyly peeking above them we know a warming trend is on the way.

Throughout January and early February we saw no mirage. No promise of any improvement in the weather.

February the 15th brought promise of our long awaited change. The first rays of the sun bounced brilliantly off the hills. They began rising higher and higher, first dark and ominous, the next vibrant and dancing. As we watched the far off Nose Hills began pushing their purple heads above the Neutrals. A warming trend was coming. Tomorrow it would be safe to dehorn Musky.

February 16th dawned clear and so warm it was almost thawing.

Musky was kept in the barn while Clarence brought the chute gates and calf cradle into the corral. It didn't take long to set them up.

Almost immediately a station wagon drove up. It was Dr. Art Schatz. He had come to do the dehorning. And get acquainted with a musk ox.

As soon as the vet nodded he was ready, Clarence opened the barn door and stepped inside. Musky ran out and went stamping down the chute and into the cradle. Rod pulled the head-gate shut, and she was caught.

Immediately Musky turned into a fire-belching tornado. If the cradle had an Achille's heel the man kneeling inches from her face fingering her horns, would be history.

Musky couldn't move her head, her body was immobilized by the cradle. Yet she managed to writhe and squirm and kick both hind feet off the ground. One got caught between the bars of the cradle, and she hung half suspended from it. But that made little difference to the energy she put into her barrage of kicks and stamps.

Fear clung to me like a leach. Musky's leg, jammed between the bars, jutted out at an unnatural angle. It looked broken. Maybe dislocated at the hip? I felt shrouded in an unnatural sense of doom. No vet could put a cast on a musk oxen that would out-last the first stamp.

Dr. Schatz was too involved with what he was doing to spare more than a cursory glance for Musky's leg. Clarence and Rod didn't seem concerned either. They were watching him.

Musky dehorned

The hair around the base of each horn had to be clipped, and the area frozen. The vet used ordinary horn-cutters to nip off each horn, carefully tying severed blood vessels before they had a chance to spurt blood. Then the horn-cavity was liberally dusted with an antibiotic that made Musky look as if she was wearing a wig.

There was scarcely any blood. Not at all like the dehornings I remembered. Musky was too worried about being caught to care about losing her horns. She probably never felt it.

The horn growth surprised us. The hollows left in her skull were the size one would expect to see when de-horning five- or six-year old cattle-beasts. The horns themselves measured thirty-six millimeters across and thirty-five millimeters long. Musky was little more than seven months, so what would her horns have been like in another year?

When Dr. Schatz finally straightened up and wiped his hands on his coveralls, Musky was panting like an exhausted dog. Her leg was still caught. Rod and Clarence had tried briefly to push it back but had given up saying "It'll come out when the cradle opens up."

Before Musky could be turned loose she had to have a shot of long-acting penicilin. She had never had a preventative dose for blackleg so this seemed a good time to give that too.

When the vet, stuffing syringe and bottles back into his bag, nodded, Rod and I helped pick up the surgical instruments scattered in the snow.

"Everyone over the fence. I'm going to let her loose." Clarence called as we finished.

We watched in anxious silence from outside the corral as Clarence quickly undid both head-gate and side door and in the same fluid movement stepped behind the chute.

Musky jerked her leg back explosively. It wasn't

broken. I let out a rush of air and breathed normally again. Musky her head held high, long hair whipping, pounded across the corral, thudding mayday stamps. But the frozen ground only echoed dull and empty sounds that quickly faded into silence.

Although her eyes glittered with naked aggression she didn't take out her anger and frustration on the fence. Nor did she come hurtling back towards where we stood behind it. I felt it would have been understandable had she wanted to wipe us from the face of the earth. But she did race back and forth along the far side of the corral, stopping often to rear up, her front feet high on the planks, nose sniffing skyward.

Had she found a way to get out Musky would have left us without a backward glance or a single ripple of regret.

That afternoon it got suddenly colder and started to snow, which wasn't good for a newly-dehorned musk ox, so Clarence put her in the barn earlier than usual. He was pleased that despite being so upset earlier in the day she had calmed down, went in willingly and started to eat immediately.

The vet didn't anticipate any trouble from the dehorning but we watched her carefully just the same. The wounds healed nicely with only a minimal amount of drainage and within a couple of weeks we felt confident there was now no danger of infection.

It would be some time before we learned the operation wasn't the complete success it appeared to be.

Chapter Fifteen

Spring and Bread Crusts

As the days lengthened winter began to lose its punch. The sun managed to melt the last of the snow from the evergreens, icicles hung like diamond-studded rapiers from every eave. The temperature, like the pendulum of a grandfather clock, swung back and forth between winter and spring.

The warmer days often found me astride a bale of straw outside Musky's corral. It was nice listening to chickadees serenading the sun while soft breezes caressed my face, causing friends to ask "Have you been south?"

But I wasn't there to get a tan, or enjoy the trilling of birds. I was there for a purpose.

If I could out-wait Musky, I hoped she would get over her time-consuming habit of rubbing her face before coming for feed. It proved a battle of patience. For what is time to a musk ox? Whereas my life was orchestrated by a mechanical watch.

I couldn't wait indefinitely, even if Musky could, so when I left, the hay left with me. True there was always feed she could help herself to, but mine was late-cut alfalfa, tender, green, and succulent. And Musky knew the difference.

It didn't take her long to learn if she wanted my alfalfa she better come quickly. Then I'd often find her waiting for me at the fence. Sometimes she'd let me reach out and rub her face. That always made her snort but it wasn't the saber-rattling snort we had become accustomed to.

She had her bad days too. Days when she would stand

back, head down, eyes wild, trying to intimidate me into throwing in the hay and leaving. When I didn't she'd stamp, snort, polish her face, then come hurtling towards me in a blazing outburst of fury. The corral planks bore the brunt of these attacks.

Some days she hit the fence repeatedly with so much venom and determination that nervous ripples raced up and down my spine. What if she splintered the planks and got out? Other days she might hit the fence once then stop and eat as calmly as if that had merely been a routine ritual. On those days she often let me reach between the planks to touch her.

I kept wondering why our musk ox was so different from the Fairbanks animals. Or was she different? Maybe it was us. Where we going about it all wrong?

Clarence tried to reassure me. "Don't expect a miracle. Give her time. Remember she's alone. In foreign territory. And we're the enemy. Sometimes quiet cattle go berserk when they find themselves in strange surroundings. Have you forgotten Daisy, our old blue milk cow? Weren't you at the auction barn the day she was sold?"

I was indeed. And remembering, I grinned like an idiot. She had sales-ring workers scattering like frightened mice, buyers scrambled for higher seats.

Our quiet milk cow was doing her darndest to stir up pandemonium in the sales area until the auctioneer shouted "Heads up boys! She's coming out." As soon as Daisy escaped from the confusion, the lights, the blare of the sales arena and got with her own kind again, she was fine.

But back to Musky. Of course Clarence was right. But if only I could find a treat she really liked surely it would help to tame her.

I remembered our friends Miles and Bee Smeeton near Cochrane, Alberta, telling us about a moose who tangled with a porcupine. It was a bottle-raised animal who normally thought he was a human. But half a ton of moose with his face bristling with quills isn't exactly a stuffed toy. So how did the Smeetons keep him still while they pulled out quills? They did it with bread.

Bee knew he loved bread crusts. She usually had a bin full. So now Miles fed the moose crusts, pushing them at him the way a thresher man forks bundles into the feeder, while Bee pulled quills faster than a farm wife plucks chickens.

Maybe a musk ox might like crusts too. I reached into my breadbox, then headed for Musky. She ate that crust, licking her lips afterwards as if she'd like another. I hadn't brought any more. She'd have to wait until tomorrow.

The next day my pocket bulged with bread. Musky wasted no time in coming up to the fence. She ate the first slice as if it was pure ambrosia . When it was eaten she reached out as if asking for another. So I gave it to her.

The bread was no sooner in her mouth than Yuk! Her lips curled in distaste and she spit it out. Then she backed away snorting venom. Was it because it had landed at her feet? Or did she think I was trying to poison her?

I swung on my heel in disgust, tossed the remaining bread onto the ground and called Rev. Our German Shepherd didn't waste any time gulping down the bread, then sniffed about for stray crumbs. Why hadn't it tasted good to Musky?

Puzzled I walked slowly to the house.

Chapter Sixteen

Moving Her Barn to Dry Ground

As the sun flexed winter-weary muscles water began oozing from honeycombed drifts. Days brilliant with March sunshine had shrunk the snow to half it's winter depth. It was heavy with water.

A prolonged thaw could flood the musk-ox corral. It was time to move Musky to higher ground.

The next day, a Saturday, she was driven into the barn at mid-day and the door shut. To make sure it stayed shut Rod drove a nail in alongside the latch.

Churchill, the front-end-loader, growled complaints as Clarence drove it towards the musk-ox corral, its wheels half submerged in a mixture of mud and slush and snow. As Rod unhinged gates which had formed the musk-ox corral, and chained them to churchill, the machine lifted them into the air, then backed away with its wheels slipping.

It didn't take long to re-locate the gates and hinge them together again into a fence. With the gates in place and at angles so they braced themselves, it was time to move the barn.

Rod fastened chains to the skids then motioned to his Dad "OK. Haul it away."

I watched, wondering how Musky would like her ride. Luckily it would be a short one. In no time she'd be out again with a new corral to explore.

But I'd forgotten about the mud. The skids were digging in like the hooves of a balky mule. Without proper footing churchill couldn't pull the barn. It's wheels turned, churned and spun, digging themselves deeper into a muddy grave. It was stuck.

Rod ran to put a battery in one of the field tractors and get it started. With both machines ramming ahead in unison, hitting the chains with a series of jerks they made some progress. But it was slow. With no traction for the machines to get down to a good steady lug it was back up, jerk, inch ahead, slip, back up, jerk again. This sort of treatment broke a skid. It pulled out.

Rod looked like a pressure cooker ready to explode, but Clarence said quietly, "We'll have to fix it."

In order to replace the skid the front-end of the barn had to be lifted and tilted at a near forty-five degree angle.

While this was going on there wasn't a sound from Musky. What was she doing? Did she think she was hanging precariously to the side of a mountain and become too scared to move?

Looking up at the window that was now far higher than its intended nine feet, I found myself wishing I was a monkey. Then I could climb up the slope of the wall and have a look. While the men pounded and pried with wrecking-bar and wedge, working to get the broken skid off, I watched. I wished Musky would make some sound. But she stayed frighteningly still.

Eventually the new skid was in place. The tractors started up again and the barn was successfully jerked into position. Soon now the men would be ready to let Musky out. She had been shut up for hours with her world tilted at a crazy angle. I hoped she was all right.

As soon as Clarence opened the barn door, Musky appeared in the doorway looking like Noah the day the sun shone. With eyes sparking interest, her head high, nostrils testing the air, she turned to us with an expression of wonderment. Where was she?

When satisfied there was no immediate danger she

gingerly lowered one foot to the ground and waited to see what would happen. When nothing did she put down the other one.

She stood that way so long we began wondering if she would ever move. When she did it was back into the barn. This was typical musk-ox behavior. When faced with a strange situation she needed to know she could back to safety if necessary.

Musky, satisfied her escape route was open, was soon back again with both front feet on the ground. She was still suspicious, as if half expecting a trap. However she eventually decided it was safe to come out. And then she moved with extreme caution investigating every blade of grass, always keeping one eye on the barn. Had the wind rustled a dried weed or a snow worm wiggled its tail she would have rushed into the barn in a flurry of stamps and snorts.

As the lengthening rays of a spent sun threw out long evening shadows she turned her attention to the planks, smelling and studying them. Only when satisfied they were the same old familiar planks, did she feel safe enough to nibble at some dried grass.

Musky's new corral was close to my clothes-line. She liked to watch me hang out the wash. When sheets billowed and danced like something alive, flapping and snapping in a brisk spring breeze, she didn't shy away from them as one might have expected. Instead she watched them as if wondering what sort of weird creatures these were.

Her curiosity seemed to outweigh any sense of fear. Which struck us as unusual in a species foreign to the ways of man. Knowing only those who carry guns that kill.

Something else seemed to fascinate Musky.

We like to work our young horses on a longe-line.

This means they circle us on a thirty-foot line, walking, trotting, and stopping on command. This sort of training instills confidence in the colt for his handler and teaches him respect and obedience while strengthening him physically by suppling his muscles. It improves his balance and is a good prelude to any type of riding.

My favourite longing ground was a grassy area near the musk-ox corral. At first Musky galloped around looking worried when I trotted the colt. But when I called "whoa" and the colt, some thirty feet from me, stopped and waited while I walked up to pet him, her eyes bulged. She watched in shocked surprise as if grappling with the question "Why hadn't the colt run away?" Then she would stand with a thoughtful expression as if trying to figure out something.

Perhaps it was only imagination, but I fancied Musky, seeing the colt had no fear of me, became a little friendlier herself.

Chapter Seventeen

Musky Takes a Bath

With the return of green-grass Musky spent a lot of time nipping off the tender new growth growing inside her corral. She watched hungrily when I pulled lush out-of-reach handfuls for her. She'd even tolerate some petting to get it.

I was now able to scratch her face, occasionally even move my hand back to fondle her ears while she was eating. But if I tried to reach beyond that she'd back off stamping, then lunge at me as if her sense of propriety had been offended.

With qiviut-gathering only a few weeks away and Musky still persisting in her "hands-off" policy, I wondered how we were going to get the wool.

I re-read Dr. Teal's statement. "Gradually breaking away from the skin, it (qiviut) works its way through the outer guard hairs and comes off in big sheets." He claimed pulling off the qiviut was easier than taking off a sweater.

It sounded simple. Except Musky didn't want anyone to touch her. Perhaps with a long handled rake we could reach out and snare the qiviut dangling from her sides.

It was easy enough now to coax Musky up to the fence with a handful of poplar leaves. However the moment Clarence tried to maneuver the rake close enough to snare a gob of wool on its teeth, Musky would snort and step out of reach. She'd come back right away for grass, but always with one eye on the rake.

There didn't seem any alternative but to put her in the

training pen. In there Clarence hoped it would be relatively easy to comb off the dangling qiviut.

It wasn't.

When a hand touched her she kicked up more ruckus than bombs exploding inside a bank vault. I tried not to listen. But there was no way to not hear it.

"It's not worth it. That animal will kill herself. Why don't you forget about qiviut this year," I urged Clarence when he came in mopping perspiration from his face. "Maybe next year she'll be quieter."

But my husband is not one to give up easily. Burpees never are. They just get a taut look around their mouth, a determined glint in their eyes and go at it again.

The wool was making Musky hot. It had to come off.

Clarence expected Musky to get used to being touched. John Teal said musk oxen enjoy being scratched and petted. Not Musky. She became more violent and harder to chase into the barn.

She was so unmanageable now Clarence had to rope and tie her to one end of the training-pen before he could touch her. Then she'd fight as only a musk ox can.

Gathering qiviut was hard work for Clarence. It was even harder on Musky. After each session she'd stand open mouthed and panting. That worried my husband. The statement "qiviut comes off as easily as taking off a sweater" seemed like the fabrication of a too fertile imagination.

I was pleased that Musky wasn't blaming me for her troubles. She'd come to eat grass or beet pellets from my hand just as before, as long as neither Rod or Clarence were in sight. When they appeared she'd run off in a humping, stiff-legged, head up, snorting gallop that left me wondering if it wasn't more defiance than fear.

When she ran qiviut danced and swayed along her sides like trophies from a scalping foray. Some fell off and became ensnarled on the rose bushes where one might assume it could be salvaged, but once shed qiviut becomes as elusive as Jason's Golden Fleece.

The Territorial Council at Yellowknife found this out to their chagrin. They reasoned that with hundreds of animals stamping across the tundra, dropping qiviut as they went, it would be plentiful. And at fifty dollars a pound, worth picking up. Accordingly, five-thousand dollars of tax-payers' money was voted to pay pickers to roam the tundra and gather qiviut.

When the money ran out the pickers returned with their wool, a scant five-pound bag from which only two pounds was acceptable quality. The remainder was infiltrated with filth. Or was old and brittle from months of continuous sunshine. Some was caribou fur, harsh and coarse. The whole operation was a farce. No wonder the Deputy Commissioner had a red face when he showed us the wool.

Our Alberta weather, trying to redeem itself for a cold January, turned unusually hot in May. Tiny leaves, exploding like popcorn, burst out on every branch, then raced each other to maturity. Mosquito wrigglers leaped from pot-holes to become blood-thirsty adults overnight. Grass shot up in record time. The sun shone with relentless persistence from cloudless skies. Shimmering heat-waves danced and spun like whirling dervishes across the fields.

We were uneasy about Musky, her coat still ragged with the remnants of her Arctic underwear. Musk oxen, with sweat glands only on their tongue and the soles of their feet, have an inadequate cooling system for blistering days.

But Musky had a unique way of coping with that problem.

At first we thought the heat had given her a raging

thirst. Her water-trough, irregardless of how often it was filled, rarely had more than a few inches of water in the bottom.

Then one day we learned why.

I saw Musky walk up to her trough, sniff the water as if about to drink, then hesitate and look around with an almost furtive air. She gave me a mental picture of a punctilious spinster peering over spectacles to make sure no one is watching before pulling off shoes and stockings, hoisting her skirts, and wading out into a cool stream.

Musky stepped into the trough with a sigh of content as her bulk sank into the cool wetness, squishing water out on all sides.

She looked the picture of bliss as she wiggled her body this way and that until all parts of it were thoroughly wet. When satisfied she was properly saturated she stepped out and walked away, leaving behind a trail of droplets that quickly evaporated on the hot ground.

I wiped sweat from my burning face with a tinge of envy as I dumped another three pails of water into her trough.

By the end of May Clarence had gathered two pounds of qiviut. There seemed no reason why he wouldn't gather the rest.

Chapter Eighteen

Pneumonia

The doctor's face was grim. "Contact your family immediately. And don't you leave town. Your husband is damn sick. Being a diabetic is against him." Then in response to the stunned look on my face he continued. "A ruptured appendix. Worse mess I've ever seen. Must've happened two days ago."

God! How could that be?

Three days ago a doctor had told my husband "It's nothing serious. Go home and don't worry about it." He hadn't. . . .

But I did. Clarence wasn't eating yet he hadn't cut back on his insulin. That should have made him a sure-fire candidate for an insulin reaction. Yet he hadn't had one. That puzzled us, especially as he is what the medical profession term a "Brittle Diabetic."

I watched him like a cat at a mouse-hole. But apart from feeling draggy, and occasionally nauseated there wasn't much one could put a finger on. There was no localized pain. He balked at going back to the doctor to be told again it was only his imagination.

The sun was a great red orb sinking into the Western horizon when Rod, his face lined with concern, came to me saying quietly. "Mum. I think you should phone Grandpa's doctor in Camrose. If you can get Dad admitted to the hospital tonight you should take him up. He's sicker than he realizes."

That was the catalyst I needed.

We reached the Camrose hospital at midnight.

Clarence hadn't looked sick enough for the admitting nurse to think it necessary to call the house doctor to do an immediate check-up. It could wait until morning. And I hadn't insisted.

At 4 a.m. Clarence complained of excruciating pain in the abdomen. A pain so terrible that had he not been in the hospital he couldn't have endured the agony of getting there. Now a few hours later I was facing widowhood.

We haunted the hospital as Clarence wavered between this world and the next. But he clung to life with such Burpee tenacity that within a week even the doctor started to wear a relieved look.

We dared to hope again.

Back at the ranch there were things to attend to. Rod jumped into the breach and finished seeding, working long, hot dusty hours after school. Terry Lee came home and between the three of us we got the late calves vaccinated, dehorned, and out to pasture. The bulls were turned out with their respective herds.

The mares were foaling and had to be checked. The stallions fed and exercised. Then there was Musky.

It was very hot. The last of her qivuit was hanging in untidy hanks, so Rod and Terry Lee decided they ought to finish taking it off. They put her into the barn and went through the usual steps of tying her before starting to comb off qiviut.

At first Musky acted as obstreperous as ever, repeatedly bashing her head into the boards. Them, as if satisfied she had made her objection clear, she stood quietly for qiviut to be combed from her right side, but threw another tantrum when her left side was touched.

But what was unusual about that? Foals who stand quietly when handled from one side, can get skittish the first time the handler moves to the opposite side. Ever try milking a cow or mounting a horse from the "wrong" side? Some won't mind. Most will. And those that do will let you know. So what was different about Musky?

Combing qiviut from her right side meant the operator had to stand on her left side and reach over her back to catch the wool dangling from her far shoulder, flank and barrel. It would have been understandable if that demoralized her. Only it didn't. It was when her left, the near side, was touched that she flew into a rage.

"What an odd-ball," muttered Rod as he handed Terry Lee the last of the qiviut. We had taken off a total of nearly four pounds of wool. Musky should feel cooler now.

* * *

I left the house to start morning chores on June l2th. A pre-dawn shower had temporarily cooled the air, made the ground steam with the earthy after-a-rain smell that makes humans involuntarily breathe deeper and drink in air as if it was a heady nectar. An eager sun was greeting the day, sparkling on the Neutrals, tossing out sunbeams laughing with promise. My husband was improving. The world was a radiant, shimmering orb.

That was before I saw Musky.

She hadn't eaten the grain given her last evening. She was lying down. Shivering. Eyes closed. Coat dull and listless. An ominous cloud swept across my mind. Blotting out all thoughts of well-being.

"Come on Musky. Get up. You aren't sick. . . .? Are you. . . .?" She gave no sign of having heard.

I pulled dandelion leaves and waved them before her calling "Hey Musky! Look." She opened one eye. Then closed it. If dandelions, her favourite, so fresh they still glistened with moisture, didn't interest her then something MUST be wrong.

Suddenly there were rocks in my stomach. Damn! Damn! Damn! Why couldn't she have waited until Clarence was better? Or if she HAD to get sick why hadn't she done it yesterday? Keith and Delbert Degenhardt would have been here then to help. Now it was just Rod, Terry Lee, and I. How were we going to cope with a sick musk oxen?

"Whoa. Slow down. Keep your cool." I told myself. "Phone the vet. Let him decide what's wrong and how to treat her." I turned and hurried to the house. But not before giving Musky another anxious look hoping I might have been mistaken. But she was shivering spasmodically and hunkered down so low she appeared to be sinking into the ground.

The veterinarian's voice sounded sleepy, but I was too worried to care. What if I had dragged him from his bed? "We've got a sick musk oxen. Can you come right away. . . . ?"

"No!" hissed Rod in my ear. "I've got to get the chute and cradle moved in before he can do anything. Tell him . . . tell him two hours."

I relayed the message.

We gulped breakfast while outlining what had to be done. The first thing was to get Musky into the barn. We didn't anticipate any trouble there.

"O.K. Musky. Get in." Rod called. She stared at him as if in a vacuum. He rapped his knuckles sharply against the plank fence. She jumped up and stamped to the far side of the corral.

Rod circled to where she stood. "Go on. Get in" The tone was commanding but Musky only snorted and pounded off to the opposite side.

She didn't look sick now. Maybe I had been mistaken.

Then I remembered one of Al Oeming's musk oxen . . . down with an unbelievably high temperature . . . 109

was the report we heard, who became amazingly active when they tried to catch it.

I pulled a handful of dandelions, and shook the oat dish too. She ignored them. Musky stood in the middle of the corral, the picture of a persecuted aristocrat, haughty and very much alone. Yet unwilling to give, or accept terms.

Eventually she might have come for oats, but with the vet due to arrive soon, and with work to be done first, we couldn't afford to spend that sort of time. Or so we thought.

So we kept trying to chase Musky in.

Rod's demands got louder, more threatening. Terry Lee and I spaced ourselves strategically so there would always be one of us near to shout and wave our arms if she ran in our direction. But it was no use. We might as well have been doing morning push-ups.

In the winter Musky had gone into the barn if pails were thrown into the corral. We decided to try using them again, and hurriedly gathered up the half-dozen or so lying near the shop.

When Rod yelled "Now!" three pails clattered simultaneously into the corral and rolled hiccuping towards her. She snorted and stamped. Circled the corral at a thumping gallop then returned to the center and stopped. Her eyes were wild now. Despite her illness (or maybe because of it) there was a stubborn, determined look about her that should have told us we were in for trouble.

We got more pails and bombarded her again. They bounced around the corral like hail stones on a July day, but she avoided them, sometimes dodging one while jumping over another with never a break in stride.

She stormed along, weaving in and out among the pails, whirling to give lightning-quick jabs at those that hit her, sending them careening off to smash against the fence, only to bounce back and increase the general confusion.

To compound the bedlam we were racing around on the outside waving our arms and pounding on whatever part of the fence was nearest to her, yelling. “Musky Get In!” It was a mad-house.

“What’s the use?” I finally croaked wearily. “She’s got us beat. I’ll go in and phone the vet not to come.”

“No!” stormed Rod. “Don’t do that. She’s so riled up now she’ll die of pneumonia for sure if we don’t treat her.”

He pushed back his sweat-stained hat and wiped the perspiration from his forehead with a grimy hand. His next words had an air of confidence I couldn’t share. “I’ll rope her.”

Suddenly I felt worn out and very tired.

My son, perched precariously astride the top rail, rope twirling, eyes deadly intent, face drawn and grim and streaked with dirty sweat, looked older than his sixteen years.

The lasso sailed out and settled over Musky’s neck. He had her. In the same instant I wished he hadn’t.

All hell broke loose.

Crashing about like a berserk hippo she kept charging to the end of the rope only to be jerked end-for-end and slammed to the ground with sickening thuds. How long could she go on punishing herself in this insane fashion?

An unhappy memory blanketed my mind like a grisly shroud. A young colt, piqued at being led away from his dam, had reared, then dashed himself to the ground. He died instantly.

A glance at Rod, his face pinched and bloodless, his knuckles white where they gripped the rope, told me he too was thinking of that colt. As if reading my mind he fed out the lasso until Musky had slack enough so now the fence, not the rope, would stop her wild charges.

She slammed into the planks with the drive of an out of control tank. Blood from her forehead splattered the fence, yet she kept charging, immune to pain, bereft of feeling.

Such passion for self-destruction was scary.

Without warning Musky turned and came streaking like a hairy cannon-ball straight towards where I stood. Involuntarily I stepped back from the fence shouting "Stop Musky! Stop!" But she hurled herself up into the air like a programmed missile.

The seven-foot high fence looked terrifyingly inadequate. For one awful moment I was sure she had made it over. Then she crumpled and fell back in a heap on the ground.

"Rod!" I screamed. "Let go the rope! She'll break her neck!" But before the words were properly out she was up and hurtling towards the other side, the lasso trailing.

Perhaps it was the trailing rope that did it. Or perhaps she had simply had enough. Instead of hitting the fence again, or trying to jump it, she swerved unexpectedly and charged through the open door.

Terry Lee had been waiting for just this. She yanked the string, the barn door slammed and Musky was shut in the barn.

Rod sagged. He put his arm against the fence and wearily leaned his head on it. Terry Lee slumped limply to the ground. My knees felt rubbery. No one spoke.

Finally Rod brought us back to reality by snorting "That's some sick-acting musk ox. If you ask me she's crazy as hell. Say . . . it's eleven o'clock! The vet should've been here an hour ago, And we're still not ready for him. I better get cracking."

Even as he spoke he was striding off to get churchill.

His face flushed from heat and exertion, a grim twist

to his mouth, Rod maneuvered the front-end-loader into tight corners, lifting cradle and chute-gates up and over the fence, then letting them down precisely where they needed to go. I was proud of our teen-age son.

"There! That ought to hold her" he snapped as the last piece was in place. "Golly! I'm hot. Sure wish the vet was here. Wonder what happened to him?" Rod wiped a dusty sleeve across his glistening face.

I started towards the house intending to phone again when Terry Lee called. "There's a car coming now Mum. Looks like his station-wagon."

"Sorry I'm late." It was Dr. Bill Crawford, big, powerful and exuding confidence with every stride." "We had trouble at the Clinic. A Charolais bull, big and mean as hell broke out and headed for down-town Wainwright. God! Talk about pandemonium.

"People flew like chickens squawking in a hail storm. They won't forget that fellow in a hurry. The boys at the Clinic won't either" he added with a wry grin. "I hope your musk ox isn't that wild. Let's have a look at her."

"D'you think she'll go in the cradle?" he asked when we told him the trouble it had been to get her into the barn.

"She'd better." Rod replied grimly.

When I offered to chase Musky out of the barn Dr. Crawford objected "It's too risky for you." But he agreed I could try when he realized I'd be behind the partition.

Now that Musky was in the barn she saw no reason to leave. She glared at me like a snarling dog.

I spoke to her and waved my arms. Nothing happened. I tried yelling and banging on the partition. Still nothing. I threw a stick and it hit her. She jumped sideways and snorted. I banged on the wall and shouted some more. She ignored that.

"Here! Let me in there! I'll make her move." and Rod

stomped into the barn thundering "Musky Get!"

She got.

She raced from the barn like a mixed-up tornado, bumping and banging the sides of the chute as she ran. But if she had hoped to escape by jumping through the calf-cradle Dr. Crawford thwarted that plan by snapping the head-gate shut.

Before Musky knew what was happening the cradle tipped and she was on her side enduring the ignominy of a thermometer in her rectum, a stethoscope sounding her heart and lungs, exploratory fingers probing.

With a temperature of 103.8 (100 is considered normal for a musk ox) and a respiration of 168, the diagnosis was pneumonia. She was given a 30 c.c. injection of Oxyvet, plus two aminebolic boluses, the latter to help perk up her appetite.

With that done we opened the end-gate to let her back out of the cradle. She shot backwards and didn't stop until her tail was tight against the far wall of the barn. Then unable to go any further she stood and glared at us.

Dr. Crawford watched her thoughtfully then said, "Give her Oxyvet for the next two days. . . . 30 c.c. per dose. The boluses I gave her will make her hungry so try to tempt her to eat. That along with good nursing is all I can recommend.

"I'll stop in again in a couple of days to see how you're making out. Good luck. Tell Clarence I'm sure sorry he's sick." With a cheery smile and a wave he was on his way. And we were on our own.

Exactly what does good nursing mean when the patient happens to be a recalcitrant musk ox, I wondered with a heavy sigh. Then I brightened a little. At least Musky wouldn't be able to tear around as she had done this morning. We'd keep her shut in the barn-chute area. If Rod widened the chute just a little she could lie in it quite comfortably when the barn got hot and stuffy.

While Rod adjusted the width of the chute Terry Lee backed the big grain-truck up so its mid-day shadow made shade for Musky. I went looking for tender saskatoon and willow twigs.

These, when pushed in front of her nose made her blink gloomily, and although she ate a few leaves it was with a complete lack of enthusiasm.

Later in the day she seemed to take a different view of life. She had a good drink of water, ate some leaves, and even nosed her grain about in a picky fashion.

Musky liked beet pellets but we had run out and couldn't get any from the dealer until tomorrow. We didn't want to wait that long.

With 4-H Achievement days over for the Beef clubs there must be a member somewhere with beet pellets left over, so I did some phoning, and finally located a 4-Her with pellets to sell. The thirty-mile trip made in spewing dust clouds seemed well worth while when Musky started right in to eat them.

I went to bed hoping by morning Musky would be better. If she wasn't and we lost her how could I break the news to Clarence? How does one tell a man his dream is ended? Finished before it got properly started.

Maybe he was still too sick to care.

Chapter Nineteen

Musky's Battle with Medical Treatment

It was a long night. Nagging thoughts crowded out sleep.

When morning finally came I dreaded going out. Memories of other dawns were still too fresh.

The exquisite Arabian filly I'd spent weeks trying to nurse back to health—her dam's anxious whinny even before I reached the barn told me I had failed. Then there was Rod's pony, Nutmeg. I found her strangled in her stall, the victim of a freak accident; or Khem, proud and beautiful Khem with blood streaming from one eye, the sight gone from it forever. I lived those mornings again. Felt the same mind-numbing sense of futility at human inadequacy to cope with tragedy and death.

Pulling on boots and reaching for a cap, the porch window drew my eyes and held them like a magnet. There was no sign of Musky.

I stepped into the early morning sunshine, forcing my feet to move towards her corral. Like machine-driven robots they made bleak, hollow echoes as they took me closer to the corral. A corral where a dark heap lay sprawled like a grotesque shadow on the ground. Fear stabbed like a knife, twisting and gouging. My mind stumbled over how to tell Clarence.

But wait. The knife did another half turn. Had something moved?

A hand impulsively brushed away the daze of cob-webs from my eyes. I blinked, and saw it again. This time there was no mistake. Musky had moved. An eyelid had fluttered, an ear had twitched to dislodge a mosquito.

"Musky! You're not dead." My voice held a rush of relief.

Her eyes opened. She looked at me with the dull, listless expression of a very old woman puzzling why she must go on living. Then she slowly pried herself up off the ground.

Having done so she stood so still I almost expected her to topple over. Dead. Eventually she shook herself with methodical care and walked over to look in her feed box.

It was then I realized my finger nails had been gouging into my palms.

By the time morning chores were finished Musky was eating in an almost normal fashion.

With June exams ahead, Rod couldn't afford to miss another day of school. Terry Lee and I could cope with routine jobs. Treating Musky would have to wait until he got home.

Anxiety gnawed at me like a chronic pain. We had to give Oxyvet to Musky on our own today.

When Rod came home from school we loaded ourselves down with hypodermic syringe, medicine, thermometer and an air of confidence we clearly didn't feel, and set out to tackle the job.

Musky surprised us by galloping down the chute and into the cradle. Terry Lee pulled the head-gate shut. Rod jabbed in the needle. I didn't have time to take a proper rectal thermometer reading because her front foot was jammed between the head-gate and frame. We wanted her out of there quickly.

As soon as her head was released she jerked her foot loose and backed away. Limping. Now what? A pulled tendon? A pinched nerve? Whatever it was we hoped it wouldn't need doctoring.

The next day Musky was still limping, but I wasn't worried about giving her a needle. We had done it yesterday without any trouble. So why not today?

But we had reckoned without Musky. She had made up her mind she'd had enough injections. There would be no more.

Despite her lame foot she'd run full tilt down the chute, but before a hoof touched the cradle she'd do a sit-down stop, a complete reversal, and head back to the barn.

Rod tried to stop her by straddling the chute where he could yell and wave his hat in her face as she raced beneath him. That made her lunge up at him snorting defiance. She knew precisely what she intended to do. And by golly no one was going to stop her from doing it.

When working cattle down a chute it's common to shove a pole either behind or in front to hold a critter until we are ready for it to move on. With spaces between every plank and numerous uprights, a pole can be used at varying heights so any animal trying to back up, or go ahead, comes up against a sturdy barrier.

We got a pole now intending to hold Musky the same way, but the solid plank construction at the bottom of both corral and chute made that impossible. It meant the pole was high enough so Musky could duck under it without a break in stride. To prevent that we filled the space between the ground and the pole with empty five-gallon grease pails. Now she jumped over the pole.

"O.K. I'll fix that." Rod snorted as he went for three more poles, then spaced them twelve, twenty-four and thirty-six inches above the first. "She won't jump that" He half turned to look at Musky with a self satisfied expression. There appeared to be no way now she could avoid going into the cradle. Oh how naïve we were.

She shot us a hostile look, a look liberally laced now

with contempt, then hit the pails a wallop that sent them flying off in every direction, ducked under the bottom pole and headed back to the barn again. Our ideas weren't working too well.

All we were doing was getting Musky thoroughly riled up again. Not good for a pneumonia patient. We weren't exactly in a church-going mood ourselves.

Rod's eyes were dark as he impatiently wiped his hand across his sweaty forehead. "Guess there's nothing for it but to get a rope and tie her." But after the other rope fiasco I thought we should try something else.

"You know those long handled, spring-triggered hypodermic syringes? Just touch the loaded syringe against an animal's flank or shoulder muscle, and presto, the job is done. That's what we need."

Rod wasn't so sure.

But I got on the phone and soon located a dealer with one. In no time Rod was back with it, loaded, and ready to go.

"O.K. Musky. This time." I thought as I held her attention with dandelion leaves.

Rod pressed the gun to her flank, the spring released, Musky jumped. And that was all.

"Darn!" Rod exploded. "It broke!" In dismay we saw the antibiotic, the same colour as beer, trickling down her long hair. The glass phial lay shattered at our feet.

"That thing's useless," Rod said in disgust as he picked up his rope. "I might as well have done this in the first place. Come on Terry Lee. Help me get her into the training pen. We'll give her the needle in there" His tone left no room for argument.

He expected to put her into the pen, drop the noose over her head, snug the rope tight to the ring at the far end of the cubicle, then give her the injection by going in with her and crowding her rear-end tight against one wall. That way she couldn't jump and break the needle.

It sounded simple. It would have worked with most animals. But not with Musky.

She didn't object to going into the pen but immediately spun around and was facing the door almost before there was time to slam it shut.

It seemed she knew unless her head was tied to the far end of the training pen, leaving her rump conveniently close to the door, there was no way she could be given a needle.

Ordinarily Musky swapped ends if anyone pointed a finger at her hindquarters. Now Terry Lee touched her rump. Nothing. She tapped it with a stick. That made Musky stamp and bash her head into the door. She had no intention of turning.

Rod took the rope and swatted her across the croup. That made her furious.

"What'll she do if you slip the rope over her head and try to pull her around," I wondered out loud. That suggestion set off such an explosion I wished I'd never mentioned it. "Take it off," I shouted, "she'll kill herself."

"Why not let her out into the barn area again? Then when she goes back into the training pen, maybe if you're ready for her, you can get her roped and tied before she switches ends."

Turning when it was Musky's idea was never a problem. As fast as we put her back in the pen she'd swap ends in an instant reverse, and be facing the door again. Then stamping and snorting she'd insist it was asking the impossible to expect her to re-turn in so narrow a space. Her act was so convincing it was almost hard not to believe her.

"It's hopeless" I fumed. "I don't know why anyone wants musk oxen. They're such stupid critters."

Terry Lee managed a laugh. "Stupid? . . . Did you say

'stupid' Mum? She's pretty darned smart if you ask me."

That broke the tension. We let Musky out, got her turned around and headed back into the training pen again.

Perhaps it was the laugh that threw Musky off guard. Back in the pen she hesitated momentarily before turning, but it was long enough for Rod to get her roped and snugged up tight. It didn't take him much longer to give her the needle and let her lose again, stamping and snorting, probably not so much from the sting of the Oxyvet as from being outwitted.

So while we had given Musky her prescribed shots we were concerned that today's exhibition might counteract the good of the medicine. Perhaps we should consider another . . . provided we could give it to her quietly. We decided to sleep on it.

The next morning Rod asked me to return the hypodermic syringe. When I did the dealer was so confident it would work, explaining a hair-breadth error in adjusting the spring had resulted in the broken phial, that I brought it home to try again.

Rod was skeptical. "Well, lemme see. . . ." He examined the gun carefully. "Could be he's right," he conceded. "Let's give it another try. Can't do more than break again I guess."

This time it lived up to the dealer's claims. Musky didn't realize she was being needled until she felt the familiar sting. Then, furious at being tricked she stamped into the barn to vent her ill-humor by taking swipes at the wall. That seemed to appease her for she soon came out again to eat the dandelion leaves I pulled for her.

While I was feeding her Dr. Crawford arrived, calling as he stepped from the car "How's Musky?" He grinned at our problems but was pleased with her progress. He had been afraid we might lose her.

"I'll leave you sulfa powder to put in her grain," he said. "If she eats it, it will be better than giving her more Oxyvet. There is danger of that destroying the bacteria in the rumen if she gets too much. Give the powder for a couple of days and then quit. She probably won't need any other medication."

That night I had the first good sleep since Clarence got sick.

Chapter Twenty

Terry Lee Takes Over Training

We had scarcely got over our scare with Musky, when I answered the phone to hear "Clarence Burpee please. Cliff Downey from Ottawa is on the line."

To my "He's not here. He's in hospital" I heard Cliff's voice: "It's OK operator. I'll speak with Mrs. Burpee. Hello Mary. Did I hear you say Clarence is in hospital? I'm sure sorry to hear that. When do you expect him home?"

"Not for two weeks. Perhaps longer."

There was dead silence at the other end, then finally—"Listen Mary, I've been talking to Commissioner Stuart Hodgson at Yellowknife. I think he's ready to consider the possibility of a musk-ox capture in August. Can Clarence phone him? Right away?"

"Gosh Cliff! Clarence is far too sick. There's no way he can plan a musk-ox expedition. Not this summer . . ." my voice trailed away as the irony of life settled like a weight in my chest.

Cliff agreed I should contact the Commissioner and explain the situation. There seemed no reason to believe he wouldn't agree to a capture next year.

Maybe Mr. Downey had been wrong in his assessment of Mr. Hodgson's thinking. Or perhaps a change in Government personnel was to colour the Territorial policy on musk oxen. But whatever the reason Clarence never got a permit to capture calves.

* * *

When my husband finally got home, walking even a few steps brought great gobs of perspiration to his face, but he insisted he must see Musky. It seemed worth the effort when Musky came up to sniff his hand.

As the summer progressed Musky continued to surprise us with her encompassing palate. She ate everything from raspberry prunings to Russian pig-weed and wild portulaca with relish and munched all sorts of woody growth like a youngster does potato chips.

Yet she had idiosyncrasies too. Lamb's quarter pig-weed, which we prefer to spinach, and carrots were on her "Yuk!" list. Yet she would eat carrot tops with gusto. Was it possible last winter's memory of the carrot fiasco still rankled? She developed an addiction to corn, often behaving badly when something else was offered as a substitute.

My parents liked to come to the ranch for summer visits. When they did Mum enjoyed pulling handfuls of green grass for the stallions, Khem and Image. They loved the attention almost as much as the grass. This year my mother was looking forward to making friends with Musky too.

Mom started by pulling the vetches growing around the apple trees. Musky floated on a gastronomic high as long as the supply lasted. When it was gone and Mother offered her green wild oats instead, Musky, snorting disapproval lunged at the fence administering a punishing wallop. Startled, Mom stepped back.

That brought a diabolical sparkle to Musky's eyes. She backed off and charged again, hitting the planks a crack that resounded like a pistol-shot in the quiet morning air.

Mom moved further back saying quietly, "You're an old silly." But for Musky it became something she did routinely whenever Mom went near her. She hit the fence with such reckless abandon the white hairs on her forehead soon took on a bloody hue.

Musky's animosity bothered Mom who liked animals. Nor did it make sense to us either.

"Carry a switch. Hit her on the nose every time she charges," we told Mom. But she couldn't bring herself to hit Musky. So she stayed away from her.

Then came the day when Musky decided to play her game with me. The first time she charged I stepped back in surprise. The next time I was ready for her with a stick. When she charged I reached through the rails and rapped her smartly on the nose. She jolted to a stop, gave me a long probing stare, then with a half-toss of her head walked up and let me pat her through the fence.

* * *

Terry Lee, a flurry of energy in blue jeans, Western boots, and an old straw hat, has a way with animals.

I've watched this wisp of a girl pick up a rebellious colt's feet and quietly trim them minutes after the same youngster had out-bluffed a two-hundred-pound professional farrier.

Could she work the same magic with a musk ox? She intended to find out.

Three weeks before the start of University Terry Lee breezed in one morning to announce "It's time something was done about Musky. I'm tired of trying to make friends with her through the fence."

"But Terry Lee" I protested ,"you could get your ribs caved in. Or a leg broken."

"Don't worry Mum. I'll keep close to the fence. Climb over fast. If I have to."

I was worried about her. So was her father. But she is a Burpee, therefore not one to give up easily. And she does have a way with animals. Here is her story:

"I didn't feel as confident as I tried to pretend. Actually I was scared. I knew Musky too well not to know there was more emotion than rationality in what I was intending to do. But although fear might mushroom inside me, it was vital it not escape. For whatever happened Musky must never sense I was afraid. So I'd have to play my hand on bluff. It worried me some that I'd never been good at poker. Or living a lie.

"I pulled an armload of her favourite weeds and carried an old broom handle . . . just in case. Letting myself into Musky's pen I knew how a lion tamer feels when entering the cage with a wildcat.

"Musky watched me from the far side of the corral. I talked to her quietly, hoping she couldn't detect undertones of panic in my voice. She began licking her lips, then ambled slowly (so slowly it seemed she would never arrive, and I almost hoped she wouldn't) towards me.

"When she reached for the weeds I reached to touch her nose. She backed up but didn't snort. That was a good sign. Soon she was reaching for a second mouthful and I was able to reach further up her face. This time she tossed her head and snorted.

"Within a few days Musky was usually waiting for me just inside the gate. But this didn't mean she wanted to be touched. In my zeal if I tried to reach too far she'd toss her head and snort. Sometimes she stamped. A stamp brought a swat with the broom handled. This served a dual purpose. It showed her such behavior was out of bounds, and it helped shrink my goose-bumps.

"A sharp swat would send her stamping angrily away. This was more disconcerting than one might think.

"When frightened or angry a musk ox gallops in short, stiff-legged ground-jolting jumps. The disturbing part of this is that they usually run only a few paces, then whirl, and come down programmed to plow back into you.

"Fortunately she never charged. Instead she'd stand and watch, then start licking her lips. This seemed similar to the saliva reaction of a dog to food. It was a sign she'd soon come back. Peacefully.

"After Musky had been disciplined with the broom handle a few times she got the idea of standing further back and reaching the weeds by stretching her neck. This put me in a quandary. To bunt me now she'd have to come ahead which would give me a split second to jump away. But it would also give momentum to her charge. There seemed small choice between those alternatives.

"When Musky stood back I could barely reach her head. As the whole purpose of this exercise was to get her used to being touched there seemed nothing for it but to half turn and hold the weeds away from her so she'd have to step close to get them

"The startling thing was she didn't hesitate to do this. I would have been happier had she shown more reluctance. Even a little fear. But no matter, the training must go on.

"The time had come to try something new. I hoped she had learned not to bunt me, but I wasn't sure. To find out I pulled some weeds she liked and some she didn't, and held them together in a tight bunch.

"As I entered the musk-ox corral icy shivers raced up and down my back. My knees felt like cold mush.

"Musky marched up as if in complete command of the situation. While she sniffed the weeds in one hand my other hand involuntarily tightened its grip on the broom-handle. I suddenly wished I'd taken time to go to the bathroom.

"When she began nosing the weeds she liked I felt braver. Before long I had enough confidence to offer her weeds she didn't like, while holding the others just out of her reach. When nothing explosive happened I felt I'd crossed an enemy mine-field. Safely. Even lamb's quarter pigweed, which she has never eaten, didn't provoke a demonstration, so I had made progress.

"Now it was time to head back to University."

Terry Lee's training made a noticeable difference in Musky. We could rumple the hair on her face, even scratch behind her ears and it was nothing to snort about.

With this change in attitude it seemed time to think about giving Musky a larger paddock.

Chapter Twenty One

Other Relations

Musky's new pasture was fenced with seven-foot high number nine link-wire, in a two-inch diamond mesh. It was strung on ten-foot pressure-treated posts set sixteen-feet apart, with a single strand heavy tension wire both top and bottom.

Ranchers seeing it were prone to exclaim, "Good God Man! Do you need a fence like THAT for a puny little musk ox?"

We probably didn't, but it had to meet Game Farm requirements.

With the new pasture fenced it was time to move Musky into it. She was shut in the barn and once more it was hauled off to a new location. By now she was accustomed to finding herself in a fresh area after each jolting ride. She had been moved several times during the summer.

However, the spaciousness of a pasture encompassing an acre of alfalfa, brome grass and a poplar bluff, seemed to cause her concern. She stood a long time in the doorway, reminding us of the boy who visits a haunted house at midnight, then suddenly wishes he was back home in bed.

When she finally screwed up enough courage to leave the barn it took nearly three hours of cautious sniffing and investigating before she felt satisfied her new pasture was safe. Then she unwound with a bang.

She sailed around and around the pasture in wild abandon, bucking, jumping, leaping, and rearing, in a fashion that would have put Austria's famed Lippizaner steeds to shame.

Head high, long hair rippling like a field of ripening oats in a strong wind, Musky seemed determined to cover every inch of her pasture in a minimum of time.

Back and forth she raced, dashing through the undergrowth, giving playful bunts to a long dead tree-trunk each time she passed until its well-rotted roots could stand no more, and the once mighty monarch went crashing to the ground.

As it fell Musky jumped and shied away in mock terror, then turned sharply and came charging back, skidding to a stop inches from the fallen trunk.

She reached out to sniff it, then apparently satisfied it was harmless she stepped closer and gave the log a push with her head. When it didn't move she backed off. Capering like a frisky filly she galloped up and cleared the trunk with the grace of an Irish hunter. Then she wheeled and jumped it again from the opposite direction.

Tiring of that game and puffing from exertion she cavorted up to where Image, Terry Lee's gray stallion, was watching her from an adjoining paddock. She feinted a charge. He snorted, shook his head and reared, pawing air. She didn't scare him. If she was challenging him he'd take her on. But Musky had no time for him now.

She was racing off again, almost too excited to know what to do next. Image stared after her in disgust.

With such an abundance of feed in her pasture, Musky was no longer dependent on us for food. Would this new independence be detrimental to our taming program?

Clarence didn't think so. Nevertheless I was pleased when she came to eat from my hand. Even though I was offering her the same weeds she had growing all around her.

Musky seemed to enjoy having Image in the adjoining

paddock. When she took her naps now it was always near where he liked to stand. In fact she developed such a crush on the young stallion, that whenever he was out of the paddock she became noticeably perturbed, galloping about and bawling in a dismal fashion.

One day Image was out of his corral for an unusually long time while a ditching machine was in there laying an underground water system.

The operator noticed Musky racing about in humping strides, her long hair billowing and swirling in a way that reminded him of black smoke roiling up from a burning oil truck. She was panting like a broken winded horse. Her eyes were wild. Her tongue was hanging out.

Worried that it was his machine causing her to panic he shut it off and went to find Clarence.

A slow smile crinkled my husband's face when he heard what Musky was doing. She wasn't frightened of the machine. She wanted to attack it. . . . Scare it. . . . Drive it off. . . . Do anything to get rid of the thing so Image could come back.

His theory proved correct. As soon as the stallion was brought to where she could see him she snorted approval and started to eat grass.

Her affection for Image was completely one-sided. None of our horses showed any interest in Musky, but she never gave up hoping. When her greetings extended in the form of guttural bawls, half-sad, half-pleading, continued to be ignored, her initial hurt look gradually became one of crafty mischievousness.

It was as if she was saying "If I can't get your attention one way, then by gosh, I'll get it another." She began trying to scare them by galloping full tilt into the link-wire fence, billowing it out with her head and making it reverberate and twang like rocks pinging on steel.

Yet she rarely did this unless there were novice riders

on the horses. Then she put so much effort into her game she'd soon be puffing with her tongue hanging out.

Perhaps in fairness, some of her behavior was frustration at not being able to join the horses and riders. Often long after they had ridden from sight, she would still be sailing around her paddock, through the trees and smashing headlong into the fence, causing it to snap like a trampoline and bounce her back and off on another whirl around the pasture.

Horses weren't the only animals on the ranch she took an interest in. Cattle intrigued her.

When Musky heard the cows bawling at calving time she would often stand head up and listening, a far away look in her eyes. Sometimes she'd call to them in a husky voice. Then wait, ears cocked hoping from out of time and distance would come a reply. We fancied she looked sad and very lonely as she waited for the recognition that never came.

One day when we were moving the range herd past her corral one of the big bulls interpreted her bawl as a challenge to his supremacy. Bellowing in his best lord-of-the-herd manner he swaggered up to her corral. Head cocked, domineeringly presenting the horn, his eyes blazed, his hooves pawed dirt. He was spoiling for a fight.

Musky watched with obvious fascination. A ton of bull didn't frighten her.

He bellowed again and threw a hoof full of dirt over his shoulder. Who was this critter? Didn't it know he was king around here. He gave his head an angry toss, and snorted a shot of fire too.

Musky didn't move.

The bull stared, blinked, then stared harder. His roaring stopped. His beady little eyes grew big and round. Who was this cocky little stranger?

Like a balloon with a slow leak, the longer he stared

the more he deflated. Finally feeling small and quite subdued, he glanced furtively around hoping no cow was witnessing his embarrassment. One was. She got an undeserved poke in the ribs for it as he slunk away. From them on if he had to pass Musky's corral he looked the other way.

Arctic wolves have been the mortal enemy of musk oxen for centuries. So when Musky arrived at Gango Ranch, Rev, our big German Shepherd, was told to keep away from the musk ox. But either Musky lacked her wild relatives' fear of wolves or she was discerning enough to know the difference between a German Shepherd and a wolf. It wasn't long until musk ox and dog were "kissing" through the fence.

Kissing was one thing. Sharing a water-trough was another. If Rev dared to try and steal a drink Musky flew at her in a rage. Rev never stayed to argue.

Should the dog follow us unnoticed into the musk-ox paddock, Musky, apart from her possessiveness over the water-trough, never paid Rev much attention. But the cat was something else again. Musky seemed to delight in scaring it. She never lost an opportunity to send it scurrying for the safety of the nearest post whenever it ventured into her paddock.

It was OK with us if Musky wanted to keep cats out of her domain, and the dog away from her drinking water. But how would she react to sharing her territory with another musk oxen? Eventually we would have to find out.

Chapter Twenty Two

Getting Musky into a Truck

Initially we had expected to take Musky to the Calgary Zoo to be bred. Bill McKay hadn't seen that as a problem. It would mean breeding daughter to sire, but incest breeding often happens in the wild. Nor did it loom as a problem in our minds. We've sometimes bred Khem's daughters back to him. When sire and dam are both near fault-free, line breeding is an important tool to produce animals with the genes to procreate themselves into future generations.

Following Musky's boute with pneumonia and Clarence's near brush with death there had seemed no hurry about getting her bred. We decided next year would be time enough. She would be bigger and better able to look after herself among strange animals.

That had been in early August. Now things looked different.

Clarence had made a spectacular recovery. Musky had developed into a fine, impressive looking animal. Perhaps we could still get her bred this fall.

My husband phoned Bill McKay, who instead of giving us the go-ahead we had expected stalled and hesitated. The decision to accept her, he said, would have to be made by the entire body of directors. He couldn't get them together for a meeting just yet. So we waited.

While waiting Clarence built a portable loading chute so he could load Musky when word came from Calgary.

"Why not crate her?" I eyed the truck skeptically. "Then you wouldn't need a loading chute."

"She'll be more comfortable in the two-ton. I'll cover the top so she can't jump out."

I didn't share my husband's confidence "How do you propose to get her up the chute and into the truck?"

I remembered a neighbour, his wife and five kids racing about shouting imprecations at each other and at the animal they chased. They were brandishing brooms and sticks, even throwing the occasional clod of earth, in a futile, sweaty effort to drive one hog up into their truck.

However, Clarence, always the optimist, didn't foresee any trouble loading Musky. To convince me he hauled the loading chute into Musky's paddock and backed the truck up to it.

In moments she was inspecting it, walking around sniffing it as she went. Testing the loading chute platform with one foot. Then another. Apparently satisfied it posed no threat she walked up it and into the truck. The whole operation had taken less than ten minutes.

Clarence grinned his "What did I tell you?" grin.

After he drove the truck away Musky continued to go up the chute. Sometimes she'd just stand there looking around. Musk oxen like the advantage of height. In the Arctic an animal will scramble up a rocky projection in an I'm-the-king-of-the-castle attitude. The rest of the herd mill below waiting for their turn to be king.

At other times Musky would gallop up the chute and without a break in stride jump down and tear off to circle the pasture, then up the chute and down again. That was a game she played in the cool of the evening.

The rut would soon be over. And still no decision from Calgary Zoo. Clarence gave up phoning. It seemed evident it was their way of saying they didn't want to breed Musky to their bull. And we couldn't entirely blame them. We were reluctant to stand out stallions at public stud because of the risk of disease brought in by outside stock.

We realized now that before another breeding season we'd have to get our own bull. But where? The prospects of getting any animals from the Territories sounded bleak.

Chapter Twenty Three

Arrival of Sandy, the Bull

Babies in the cabbage patch? Snow balls in a blast furnace? A musk ox in San Francisco? Don't be ridiculous.

Never-the-less there was a bull calf for sale at the San Francisco zoo. And Clarence spoke for him. Then began the hassle of getting him into Canada.

Initially we were told we couldn't. Impossible. There were Government restrictions banning animals entering Canada from any State having had an outbreak of either Bluetongue or Anaplasmosis within the last twelve months. California was such a State. Things looked bleak.

Then Clarence found out there were no restrictions against shipping livestock from California to Montana. Montana didn't have an Anaplasmosis or Bluetongue problem. So all we had to do was find a resident there who would look after an animal for a few weeks. It sounded simple when said fast. Not so simple if that animal happened to be a musk ox.

Then out of the blue a casual acquaintance came to volunteer his brother's services and facilities in Montana. We were over hurdle number one.

Needing to make certain what we planned to do would meet import requirements, Clarence phoned the Dominion Veterinarian again. The man he had first spoken to was away, so he had to talk to someone else. This man saw no problem arising out of our plan "But why stop in Montana?" he wanted to know. "Why not bring him right to Alberta?"

"You mean I can do that?" Clarence gasped.

"I certainly don't see why not." was the reply. "I'll get the veterinarian at Ottawa to send you a letter confirming it. Just get the animal tested for Bluetongue and Anaplasmosis, also Tuberculosis and Brucellosis, and get him into Alberta within a month of having the blood drawn and there'll be no problem."

Wow! Now things were starting to roll.

Next Clarence contacted the airlines. Yes, they could fly a crated musk oxen from San Francisco to Edmonton. And at a reasonable price.

Phone lines between Gango Ranch and San Francisco Zoo hummed and by December 29th the final count-down had started. The musk ox was scheduled to leave San Francisco airport at 4 p.m. their time, change planes in Seattle, and arrive in Edmonton's International at l a.m on the 30th.

Clarence and Rod were already on their way to the airport when a call came from San Francisco. "Mr. Burpee please."

Oh good! That's to say the musk ox is on his way. My spirits sang as I murmured "Mr. Burpee isn't home. May I take a message?"

Then came a voice I recognized "Oh Damn! I was afraid of that?" The voice belonged to Sandy, the Zoo Manager's private secretary. My heart sank faster than a rock in a bathtub.

"Mrs. Burpee, we've come up against a snag. The airline here won't bill the musk ox any further than Seattle, and we can't get assurance he can get a flight out of there. Unless it's to Toronto or Winnipeg. And that's no good. . . . ?" Her voice trailed into a question for to a girl unfamiliar with Canadian geography there seemed a chance he might be re-routed to Winnipeg.

"How come?" I gasped. "I thought you had everything checked out for a flight to Edmonton. What happened?

Where is the musk ox now?"

"He's on his way back to the zoo. We thought everything was arranged for a flight to Edmonton too. Until the crate arrived at the airport. Then they started re-checking and found the only places he can get to are Toronto and Winnipeg."

"Well, neither one of those will do!" I snapped.

She sounded contrite. "I'm really awfully sorry. I'll start checking other airlines right away. Perhaps one of them can take a musk ox. For now all we can do is wait. Tell Clarence how badly we feel about this."

Well, they weren't the only ones. How did she think we felt?

Frustration followed frustration for Clarence and Sandy, each trying to arrange a flight for a musk ox from Seattle to Edmonton. Harassed by contradictory information, plagued by bum leads, they were near their wits end.

In the year 1973 when countless tons of freight go winging to every part of the globe it seemed incredible a crated musk ox, total weight less than two-hundred-and-fifty pounds, should pose such a transportation difficulty. But it was a cold hard fact.

If Clarence wanted his musk ox he'd have to drive to Seattle and get him. Ernie McDevitt from Edmonton would go with him to share the driving so the trip home could be made non-stop. But now there was another problem.

Too much time had elapsed between the drawing of the blood and the completion of the tests for Bluetongue and Anaplasmosis for the musk ox to comply with the thirty-day importation deadline. Somebody had goofed.

The whole bloody business of tests had to be started all over again. This time the zoo people, veterinarians, everyone concerned, realized the importance of haste. With tests that take three full weeks to complete there was no time for dilly-dallying. When the count-down said blast-off everyone better be ready to blast.

Musky and Sandy, a yearling musk ox new arrival

January 30th Sandy MacTeer phoned Clarence to say "It's 'go' for shipping your musk ox on February lst from San Franciso. He'll arrive in Seattle at 2.30 that afternoon on a Flying Tiger."

"OK I'll be there." And he was.

When the musk ox, which Clarence had named Sandy, arrived at Gango Ranch his hair was short and skimpy, he only weighed ninety pounds, whereas Musky at the same age balanced the scales at two hundred and fifty. But he looked healthy so we hoped for the best. On the plus side he wasn't as wild as Musky had been on her arrival.

Sandy's eyes blazed with excitement when he saw Musky. She, standing proud and aloof, pretended not to see him. Whereas he, not understanding her keep-your-distance message, ran up to get acquainted. Then wasn't quick enough to avoid the swipe she aimed at him. But he was a fast learner.

From then on he stayed close to her rump where her head couldn't reach him unless she turned. Then he turned too. His movements were so synchronized with hers that she was rarely able to bunt him now. Eventually Musky gave up trying to drive him away. Instead she ignored him. As one would a troublesome shadow.

Clarence Burpee, and his son-in-law, John Lea of Fairview, feed oats to Musky and Sandy.

Musky would stalk about like the Queen of Sheba, her long skirts flouncing and Sandy pattering alongside her like a friendly poodle.

Eventually she must have felt flattered by his devotion. She began looking as if she enjoyed having Sandy beside her. Except at feeding time.

She became so bossy, gobbling up her grain, then chasing Sandy away from his, that Clarence had to separate them at feeding time. Even so Musky wolfed her feed, then looked for a way to eat Sandy's too.

Her greediness made it hard to make friends with Sandy because whenever we tried to coax him to the fence with feed, Musky got there first. If I dropped a handful for her then moved further on with another for Sandy, she'd dash back and forth between the piles, glaring at Sandy if he seemed on the verge of coming closer.

Sandy's arrival seemed to give Musky confidence. We could rub her back, her flanks, and even under her belly now. But only when she was eating.

When Clarence took visitors into the musk-ox paddock both animals would come together to stand squarely in front of the strangers, staring up at them as if asking "and who might you be?" But if anyone tried to pet them they'd stamp and back away.

Before we owned Gango Ranch the poplar bush in what was now the musk-ox paddock had been used as a garbage dump. A variety of ancient relics . . . tin cans, scraps of rusty metal, barbed wire, broken harness, old saucepans, and broken garden tools, had all lain hidden for years under grass, leaves, and rotting logs. Now that the musk oxen had eaten much of the underbrush and tramped down the grass it was coming to light again.

Clarence was anxious to get the junk moved away. It

looked untidy and some of it might be sharp enough to cut a musk ox.

On a week-end when the hoarfrost was loosening its hold on the trees and silently floating down to land with muffled plops on the snow below, Clarence decided it was warm enough to start the clean-up job.

Besides, this week-end he would have extra help. Terry Lee and Keith and Keith's little sister, Shelly, were down and they were ready to share in whatever ranch work was going on.

My husband brought the front-end-loader into the musk-ox paddock. Everyone began to pile whatever trash they could pull up out of the snow onto it. It was a weird looking assortment: an old walking plow frame, a knotter off a horse-drawn binder, a Tettley's tea can, a cracked vinegar jug, sealers grown blue with age, an old stoneware churn, and a conglomeration of tin cans. Barbed wire and straggly ends of mesh-wire had to be cut away and disentangled from among the fallen trees.

One would never have guessed such a harmless looking poplar bluff could hide such a motley assortment of junk.

In addition to cleaning out the trash, the crew neatly piled dead wood so it could easily be picked up by the front-end loader and hauled to the stock-tank heater.

Sandy wasn't interested in what was going on. He was too busy grubbing around where the snow had been disturbed looking for raspberry canes. Not Musky. She thought the people looked as if they were having fun. And she intended to share it.

She hovered around Shelly (perhaps because she was the smallest) like a sales-hungry store clerk. When the girl wrestled with one end of a log Musky often put her head against the other end and gave it a shove. Shelly laughed and thought this was great, but I wondered if the musk ox might be getting too friendly. What if she decided Shelly would benefit from a shove or two?

But when I cautioned Clarence to keep an eye on them he only said crossly. "Why are you always expecting trouble?"

Before the job was finished, the gang came in for coffee, leaving behind a neat pile of wood to be hauled away after lunch.

When the workers returned to the paddock they found their carefully piled poles looking like the jumbled mish-mash of river logs that had been caught in a white-water whirl pool. Musky standing proudly beside the tangled mess seemed to be admiring her accomplishments.

* * *

Towards spring Sandy was dehorned. Just as with Musky the veterinarian used Lidocaine to freeze around the base of the horn. There was little bleeding and no noticeable set-back. At the time we believed this operation too was a complete success,

Periodically Clarence had been sending samples of Musky's feces away to be examined for signs of worms or other internal parasites. Now samples from Sandy were sent away too.

When Sandy's report came back it said he had traces of Trichuris, a specie of wet-worm that lives in the last portion of the intestine and causes unthriftiness, even diarrhea.

Dr. Crawford recommended a 30 c.c. injection of Neguvon as the control measure for this type of worm.

That sounded a bit drastic. Neguvon is the systemic cattlemen pour on the backs of cows to kill warble grubs embedded in bovine tissues and vital organs. Even when used externally it sometimes causes the animal to have a reaction.

However Dr. Crawford didn't anticipate any trouble with Neguvon, but he did agree there is always an element of danger. He cautioned Clarence to phone him immediately if there were any indications of a reaction.

Before giving Sandy the Neguvon we tried out something else that was new. Clarence thought, and the vet agreed with him, that it would be a good idea to feed a little tranquilizer to the animal before he had to be needled.

After Sandy had been given Atrovet and it had started to make him dopey. Clarence and Rod put him into the squeeze and gave him the shot of Neguvon. As he walked away he seemed unsteady, but not realizing a reaction would start instantaneously, they blamed the tranquilizer.

It was calving time and the men had to go immediately to help a heifer having a delivery problem.

Half-an-hour later when I looked at Sandy he was in bad trouble. His muscles lacked co-ordination and he moved with the gait of a perennial tippler. I ran yelling for the men.

Sandy got worse quickly, staggering badly and foaming from the mouth. I rushed to phone the Vet Clinic.

"Sandy has a reaction. He's . . ."

Dr. Crawford's voice cut me off. "I'll be right down," and the receiver banged.

Sandy was suffocating. Panting in quick convulsive gasps and drooling profusely, he was dying from lack of air.

Clarence and Rod were hurriedly debating whether they should try to give him emergency oxygen from the tank on the acetylene welder, when the vet's station wagon roared into the yard. He was out and running almost before it stopped, a syringe in his hand.

Sandy lurched into an unsteady gallop, stumbling as

he ran. Dr. Crawford made the flying tackle that had earned him fame with the Calgary Stampeders, and even as he landed was jabbing a syringe full of atrophine into the musk oxen's flank.

In seconds Sandy showed signs of responding.

His breathing improved, his muscle co-ordination began to return. The vet watched him closely for half an hour then seemed satisfied, saying "You may have to give him injections every two hours. Or this one may do the trick. Keep an eye on him and see how he acts. I'll leave this bottle . . . 2 c.c.'s every hour if necessary. Call me again if you need me." And with that he was off.

Rod rubbing his chin looked impressed "That's got to be the fastest trip anyone ever made from Wainwright."

Clarence's voice sounded as tense as a stretched elastic band when he replied. "There wasn't much time."

And indeed there hadn't been.

Sandy continued to improve. By bed-time it was hard to realize we had been so close to losing him.

Chapter Twenty Four

Musk Oxen Games

The evenings were getting balmy. The tinkle of water trickling merrily away from shrinking snowdrifts was music to our ears. Miniature rivers dammed up by straws and twigs backed up into tiny lakes, then broke free in a gurgling rush of white water that brought a sparkle of hope to winter-weary eyes.

Grey pussies on the willows were growing sleek and fat on sun-warmed sap. Swelling poplar buds were beginning their metamorphosis from bud to catkin to leaf. Spring was really on its way.

In the musk-ox pasture a few stubborn rhubarb roots, missed last fall when we dug up the patch, began to show signs of life. As fast as the leaves poked above the ground the musk oxen nipped them off. This concerned us.

Rhubarb leaves contain cyanide poison and it is accumulative. Animals eating them consistently could eventually become poisoned. As soon as the ground thawed enough I took a shovel and pail intending to dig up the roots and cart them away. I hadn't reckoned with the ground being packed so hard it resembled cement. Clarence would have to bring in a machine to loosen the soil before I could dig out any but the shallower roots.

While I worked away at those Musky came to watch. Each time there were a few roots in the pail she'd give it a sly bunt that sent it rolling across the ground, spilling its contents as it went. Then she'd follow it frisking and prancing like a playful puppy, nudging it each time it started to slow down.

"Hey! Musky! Leave that pail alone," and she'd back off looking puzzled. As she watched me re-gather the scattered roots I got the feeling she was wondering how I'd look rolling across the ground. I kept the shovel handy, . . . just in case she decided to find out.

With the lengthening days the songs of robins and meadowlarks brightened our mornings while in the evening a concert of frogs arose from every slough to tell us spring had arrived.

The musk oxen spent more time lying in the shade now, but when evening brought a chill to the air they shook off their lethargy to play.

An old tractor tire which Clarence had hung from a poplar tree in their paddock became their favourite sparring partner. They would take turns charging into it, making it swing like a panic-stricken pendulum. Then they would wheel and deliberately stand so it would smack into their hind end. That was the signal to whirl and go for it again. Their hooves continually digging in for a more forceful attack wore away the ground, leaving a depression like a buffalo wallow.

They had other games they liked to play. One was follow-the-leader. They'd go crashing through the brush, splash across a slough sending sheets of water flying out like spray from a racing boat, stop briefly to shake the moisture from waterlogged coats, then off again bucking and frisking towards the tire. But instead of bunting it they would jump through it, then whirl to watch as the other came sailing after.

The musk ox liked an audience. If they knew we were watching they put more enthusiasm into their play. Sometimes they had a pretend battle, charging as if determined to shatter their skulls, only to come to a jolting stop a hair-breadth before contact. Then with a playful snort they were apt to back off and do it all over again.

When the poplars started to leaf out in mid-May their delicate pale green leaves quickly grew in size and deepened in colour. The musk ox ate them as part of their daily diet. This strengthened Clarence's belief that musk oxen would keep unwanted brush under control, even in pastures lush with alfalfa and grasses.

After eating the easy-to-reach branches they started pushing down trees up to fourteen-feet high and two inches in diameter. They did this by leaning a shoulder into the tree and pushing. As the tree starts to bend they push it still further by straddling the trunk and moving up it, eating leaves as they go. In a remarkably short time what had been a thick poplar bluff looked as if a tornado had ripped through it.

Ranchers seeing the musk oxen eat brush the way a hungry camel stuffs down hay would chew thoughtfully on a straw for a while and then with an air of having made an astonishing discovery lean towards Clarence and say in a confiding tone. "Hell! Put a few of those critters in a pasture and there wouldn't be a brush problem."

By the time the poplar leaves had turned a deep green Musky's qiviut had loosened its hold on her skin making her look as if her coat were in tatters. Sandy reminded us of a worn-out teddy-bear with its stuffing coming out.

Musky's front quarters started shedding first. This year Clarence was able to pull the wool off in large flakes as she ate. By the time her rump and back legs were shedding he could walk up behind her and comb it off with a mane-and-tail comb.

There was none of the terror or the fight of the year before. She didn't even bother to look up from grazing. Such a display of trust was the highest compliment a musk ox could pay.

With time and patience Clarence hoped he could win Sandy's trust and confidence too.

Chapter Twenty Five

Farewell to Musky

If musk oxen were to become successful ranch animals they must eventually learn to respect wire fences. Almost certainly this would come about by selective breeding, but it would take time. Clarence wanted to find out now how his pair would react to a single-strand electric fence.

He only had to set a few posts in order to string an electric fence that would divide the musk-ox paddock in two.

By late afternoon on June 21st Musky and Sandy were in the north half of their pasture. The electric wire was activated. Clarence stood back to watch.

Just as he had expected both animals immediately walked up to investigate the fence. They sniffed the wire and got a mild shock that sent them backing away snorting "danger."

Clarence's face glowed, but I couldn't rid myself of a niggling feeling we might be charting a calamity course. What if in their evening romps they forgot about the fence? Yet what real harm could there be if they did? If they ran into it the wire would certainly break, but it wasn't as if the musk oxen could get out. They would still be in the paddock.

The possibility of them getting cut never entered my head. If it had I'd have thought "No way. Their hides are tougher than old bull leather."

When the grey blue dusk of evening had slipped into the semi-darkness of a June night Clarence went to check once more on the musk oxen. This time he found them grazing quietly, one on either side of the broken wire. Musky had a nick on her face, but it looked nothing more than a scratch. Nothing like the gashes horses sometimes get when wire-cut, so we didn't give it much thought.

The next morning the damaged wire was repaired and the current switched back on. All that day the musk oxen stayed away from it, and by evening remembered to avoid it in their twilight gallops.

Several days later Clarence, his weathered face tight with anxiety, his voice terse, came in asking "Where's that antiseptic powder you use when a horse gets cut? Musky's scratch is festering. I'll have to try and treat it."

Musky wasn't a good patient. She persisted in shaking her head at the exact moment Clarence aimed a squirt of powder at the cut, and that coupled with the long hair around the scratch stopped most of the antiseptic from reaching its mark. However, by pulling down a poplar branch so she had to reach for it at an angle, Clarence was able to get one good dusting of powder into the sore. But only one for she wasn't about to fall for that trick again. Yet there seemed no reason for concern. We had seen far worse gashes heal without leaving a scar on thin-skinned Arabians.

A few evenings later I was picking raspberries from the patch near the musk-ox paddock. Musky was lying down in a way that jostled my brain into an apprehensive flutter. Was it imagination? Or was there something wrong with her? To find out I broke off a few raspberry branches and poked them through the fence calling. "Here Musky." She had a passion for raspberry leaves.

Her ears twitched but it seemed too much trouble to get up. Sandy, never one to miss an opportunity, came on the run. Listening to him eating HER leaves eventually became more than Musky could endure. She heaved herself to her feet and shuffled towards the fence. Ordinarily she would have lost no time bunting Sandy away to appropriate the leaves for herself. Now she stood a little apart with a dejected. "I don't really give a hang" look.

When Sandy, having finished eating capered up to her inviting her to come and play her reply was to lie down right where she was, too listless to bother walking back to her favourite bedding down spot.

The next morning Musky moved sluggishly towards her feed looking so gaunt her sides seemed to have fallen into hollow caverns. She didn't have the energy to threaten Sandy when he moved in to finish her oats.

I suggested a shot of penicillin, the stockman's cure-all when he doesn't know what ails a critter

However, Clarence wanting to do what was best for his musk ox, phoned the vet to come and give Musky a thorough examination.

Rod was writing June exams so we'd need extra help. A neighbouring rancher, Allan Currier, came with his eighteen-year-old son, Gordon. His wife and daughter came too.

We women sat and visited in the shade of the corral, out of the aching glare of a sun that blazed mercilessly down from a near-cloudless sky. There was scarcely a breathe of air to bring whispered relief to burning bodies. Every few minutes we'd get a tickle on our nose, brush at it and feel nothing. It was the poplar fuzz floating down to coat the land with a June "snow-storm."

Musky found a shady spot too and in a detached way watched the men enlarge the calf-cradle.

Earlier in the morning I had picked a big armload of wild raspberry canes. It had seemed a good omen when Musky showed some interest in them. Thinking they would be useful to coax her into the cradle I had stopped feeding her. They were lying in the grass beside me now.

When Art Shatz, the veterinarian arrived he walked a few steps towards Musky, looking at her with observant eyes. She lunged to her feet and stamped off. But she only went a few feet, then stopped, panting heavily.

It was a stifling day, hot enough to send rattlesnakes looking for a cool dark hiding place. Even so we didn't think Musky should pant with so little exertion.

When I tried to coax her into the calf cradle she started to come, then stopped, her eyes shifting uneasily from raspberry canes to people. Finally as if having made up her mind she gave a sickly snort and moved back into the shade.

"We'll have to chase her in." Clarence said, "but let's see if we can do it quietly. I don't want her excited."

The men climbed down off the fence and started slowly converging on her from different directions. She looked around, head up and startled.

The next moment she was stamping off, thumping towards the barn like a scared rabbit. It looked to Gordon as if she had him in her sights. He turned and raced for his recently vacated perch on the fence like a rooster flying from an axe. His feet never seemed quite able to catch up with his outstretched head. He jumped to safety just as Musky dashed on past and into the barn, completely unaware she had been the cause of the boy's record-breaking burst of speed.

Gordon's face turned fiery red, not all caused by heat and exertion, as he laughed self-consciously. "It looked safer up here."

Gordon is a young man who doesn't hesitate about dropping off a racing horse to put a ribbon on a steer's horn. He enters wild-cow-milking contests at local rodeos and acts as a no-nonsense bouncer at school dances. Yet it was no surprise to us that Musky's stamp had given him a sudden and compelling urge to climb back up on the fence. A musk-ox stamp does that to people. Even the bravest.

The next time the men closed in on Musky she turned and ran down the chute and into the cradle. There was no chasing to excite her. Yet when the veterinarian took her temperature it was 107.5 F

"God!" ejaculated Allen, "She must be a helluv a lot sicker than she looks."

I turned to Clarence voicing the question on both our minds. "Could it be a build-up of poison from eating rhubarb leaves?" No one bothered to answer.

The vet listened to her heart and lungs and scratched his chin. He was puzzled.

He wanted a closer look at her wire-cut. In order to do this Musky's head would have to be held immobile. She, already feeling victimized, had no intention of putting her head into a vice.

When the men tried to push her forward she pushed back with the perversity of a wayward mule, stamping and snorting as only a musk ox can.

Almost immediately Clarence turned to me. "See if you can tempt her in with those raspberry leaves."

I knelt down in front of the calf-cradle and shaking the leaves called softly. "Here Musky."

She lunged at me with the speed of a striking rattlesnake, her mane stiff as the hackles of a German Shepherd challenging a night prowler. Her eyes were full of hate.

At that moment the head-gate slammed shut. She was caught.

Now that the vet could examine the scratch more carefully he found it deeper than it looked and still festering. He dusted it liberally with an antibiotic.

Suddenly Musky was breathing hard. Her eyes lost their fire. She began to look dazed.

She was worried at being caught. Furious with me for what must seem like a betrayal of trust. Yet apart for throwing her head when she lunged at me, she hadn't banged around at all. There didn't seem any reason for undue concern.

With the cut taken care of and a blood-sample drawn, we climbed back up on the fence. The men opened the cradle door and released the head-gate expecting Musky to back out and run stamping across the pasture to rejoin Sandy. Instead she gave a sobbing gasp and rolled out onto the ground.

"She's dead!" a voice whispered incredulously. It wasn't until stunned faces turned towards me that I realized the words were mine.

"No. She's just choked down," the vet said. "She'll come around in a minute" And Allan agreed with him. There was the almost inaudible sound of people daring to breathe again.

To be doing something . . . anything was better than just standing. . . . I ran for a pail of water to splash over her head. Clarence and Allan, with the same urge to be doing something, went for a truck tarpaulin and started rigging it up to protect her from the merciless hammering of the sun. The vet got out his stethoscope again.

Musky's breath came in great tearing gasps, her legs sticking out like poles, one at each corner, jerked grotesquely to the fractured rhythm of her breathing as she fought for air. I kept pouring water on her head and pleading, "Come on Musky. Wake up."

The vet gave her adrenalin but the sobbing became weaker, more irregular, then slower . . . slower.

He tried artificial respiration, kneading her sides, pummeling, pounding, but only her legs responded, jerking to the cadence of his kneading.

Musky's eyes were closed. Flies were already collecting around her half-open mouth. Numbly I brushed them away, stroked her muzzle, felt the silky smoothness of her coat, the flesh beneath. She was fat. Dully I looked at the soles of her feet. Where were the sweat glands?

Clarence and Allen still struggled with the tarp as if Musky's life hinged on their efforts to give her shade. The others stood like stone, staring at the dark shape on the ground. Hope was draining away. Slowly at first. Then quickly like a gushing fountain, leaving behind only a cold, numb dread.

Oh God! Wasn't there something somebody could do?

Musky kicked spasmodically, gave a great shuddering sigh. And was still.

The tarp could come down now.

* * *

I brushed a hand across the back of my neck. It came away streaked with blood. Mosquitoes. I hadn't felt them.

There were voices. A million miles away. Asking "What happened? She should have come around."

"Hell! I've seen lots of cows . . . horses too. . . choked down a damn sight worse than that, and snap right out if it" Allan's voice rumbled. The vet was puzzled too.

"You have insurance . . . ?" the question was asked hopefully.

Numbly I shook my head.

God! That's rough." Allen aimed a squirt of tobacco juice, tumbling a beetle from a blade of grass.

We stood in a semi-circle around the stiffening body, each wrapped in our own grim thoughts. No one moved or spoke. Only the mosquitoes and flies kept up their incessant buzzing, and poplar fuzz continued to pollute the air.

When I dragged my eyes away from Musky to look at

Clarence his face was ashen and glistening with sweat. Suddenly he looked old and tired as if he had already lived a million years. There was a stricken tautness about him as if his nerves were shrieking beneath his skin. He had just lost a musk ox. And a dream.

But what the heck. It wasn't the end of the world. There would be other dreams. Maybe other musk oxen. Right now the thing my husband needed most was food.

"Musky's dead," I announced with flat finality. "Standing here isn't going to bring her back. I'm going to make sandwiches and coffee. It's past noon."

With the same reluctance to intrude as if there had been a death in the family, the Curriers wouldn't stop. The vet did. He too felt shaken.

After lunch, as the ghastly grey color left Clarence's face and his blood-sugar got back to normal, we talked.

What had really killed Musky? Rhubarb leaves? An infected cut? Had she strangled herself. Or did she die of shock. None of those things seemed likely. Yet she was dead.

"Perhaps I should have done it the easy way and given her a shot of penicillin" Clarence's eyes were dark with remorse. "Whatever happened it couldn't be worse than it is now."

"Yes it could" I struggled to be positive despite our common misery, "You have the satisfaction of knowing you did what you believed was best. That's all anyone can do. Now stop blaming yourself."

Chapter Twenty Six

Sandy and Porcupine Quills

The vet, Clarence too, wanted an autopsy. They hoped that would solve the mystery of why Musky had died.

When they went to take her remains to the Vet Clinic they found Sandy hovering over her. He sidled away watching closely as Musky's body was hoisted into the back of the half-ton. Then, as if suddenly realizing she was leaving and mightn't be back, he rushed up as if intending to jump in and go with her. The end-gate was already closed and the truck moving off but he ran after it until a gate clanged shut in his face.

As the truck faded into swirling dust patterns he gave a long, lonely bawl, a pathetic farewell to the only real friend he ever had. Without any warning my throat developed an aching tightness. I had to brush at my eyes to see to fasten the gate.

The autopsy found Musky's death the result of a ruptured blood vessel back of her brain. Perhaps from a bang? A blow on the head? She had bumped it against the top of the cradle when she lunged at me, but it had seemed like a very little bump for an animal who uses its head as a battering ram.

"Perhaps," the vet said groping for some sort of explanation that would satisfy us, "her high temperature weakened a blood vessel and made it rupture."

"But the high temperature? What caused that?" The vet gloomily shook his head and couldn't answer.

So the question hung on the horizons of our minds like a dark and dangerous funnel-cloud.

I remembered the electric fence. The foreboding. The presentiment I had stifled the day Clarence turned on the current. And wished. . . . But it was too late for that now. Dwelling on the "if only's" the "might have been" makes life too brutal.

For days Sandy drooped like uncut wheat after a wet September snow storm. He haunted the spot where Musky had died, pawing the ground as if he was hoping to conjure up a genie-of-the-lamp to restore Musky to him. But no magic wraith appeared.

Although he was facing a life-time of loneliness he never refused to eat. That surprised, and pleased, us.

One of Al Oeming's healthy musk oxen had gone on a hunger strike when a sick companion was taken away for treatment. The supposedly healthy animal caused Al nearly as much concern as did the ailing one.

Sandy looked such a forlorn, lonely little creature that I made a point of feeding him tidbits through the fence. Gradually the misery faded from his eyes. Now when I picked raspberries alongside his paddock he'd leave the shade to follow me, even on days so hot the horizon melted and ran.

I supposed the raspberry leaves I pushed through to him were the attraction. . . . Yet he had wild ones in his pasture he could eat at will. And they were in the shade. So why where mine so special?

When I parted the canes to pick low-growing berries there were times Sandy's head was almost touching mine. I wasn't sure I liked this. What if he suddenly decided to use his head as a battering ram. The link-wire would stretch and billow like a wind-filled sail, giving me almost no protection. When these thoughts crossed my mind I'd move away and pick berries a safer distance from the fence. Maybe I was being too cautious. Sandy seemed as friendly as a puppy.

Unlike Musky, the bull never showed any interest in the stallion, Image. He'd "kiss" our German Shepherd bitch but ignore Jomo the Border collie dog on the ranch.

Sandy not upset by the German Shepherd

This started us wondering if he could distinguish between the sexes in humans. And if so did it make a difference?

A rutting bull moose at Smeeton's Game Farm near Cochrane, Alberta, not only knew the difference between men and women, he made it very clear he didn't want men in what he considered HIS territory.

I found that out the fall we visited Miles and Bee Smeeton. On earlier visits their bottle-raised moose had seemed more like a massive dog than a wild animal. This time he came crashing through the underbrush, pawing dirt, snorting venom, and hooking at the mesh-wire fence near where Miles and Clarence were quietly talking. His powerful antlers would have torn the fence into twisted rubble if the men hadn't quickly moved away. When they did he side-stepped to where Bee and I were standing, all his aggression gone. He actually appeared to grin when she reached through the fence to pat his ugly face and scratch his ears.

A frost the night of September 15th finished my cucumbers. Even those under a blanket. But all thoughts of frost damage to crops or garden were swept away when Clarence came in saying. "Sandy's got porcupine quills."

Thoughts of Rev, her face bristling like a dressmaker's pin-cushion, flashed through my mind. . . . Rev has such an overwhelming hatred of the spiny rodents who occasionally wander nocturnally through our yard that the instinct to protect her family brings such a rush of adrenalin she forgets caution. And past experiences.

Our gentle German Shepherd ordinarily sits, heels, does all the things a well trained dog should do. But that vanishes when we have to pull quills from her face. She'll sit stoically to endure the pulling of the first half dozen quills. After that her patience snaps. Pliers or fingers zeroing in on a quill changes her into seventy pounds of writhing, threshing, snarling resistance. Clarence, big man as he is, can't hold her still. We have to give her ether to get the quills out.

Ether to a musk ox? We weren't prepared for that sort of experiment. And we weren't any happier about the thought of putting him in the calf cradle. Not after what had happened to Musky.

"There's a chance I can pull them out while he's eating" Clarence said hopefully.

"You aren't likely to get far with that." I snorted. Not long ago I had tried to sweet-talk a mare into letting me pull a half-dozen quills from her tea-cup muzzle when I didn't have either rope or halter with me. She was a gentle, people-loving Arabian but she didn't go for that idea at all.

However, when Clarence tried the oats he did pull out a few quills. But pulling them hurt so Sandy soon had enough of that. We were going to have to think of some other way.

Allen Currier came again and brought his lasso plus three helpers. He twirled the rope and it settled neatly over Sandy's neck. Quick as a flash another rope twirled and had him by the back leg. An expert twist laid Sandy neatly on the ground, stretched out flat and helpless.

Two men held the ropes snug while Allen kneeling on Sandy's neck, helped Clarence pull quills. They opened his mouth but unlike Rev, Sandy only had quills on the outside. However, because of his long hair those had to be felt rather than seen. Every inch of his face and legs had to be explored with careful fingers. Even a tiny broken off stump could fester and cause trouble.

No animal likes being forcibly held down. At first Sandy's eyes rolled with terrible, roiling anger when he had to submit to fingers probing for quills. Sometimes he theshed about in an attempt to jerk his feet free of the ropes. But for the most part he lay quietly, almost as if in spite of himself he was grateful to the men helping him.

Allen, with years of experience handling range cattle and horses, was impressed at how quietly the musk ox behaved.

When the quills were out and the ropes taken off the musk ox jumped up. He backed off, head down as if ready to plow into the first person who moved. However, when the men walked off he watched for a moment then followed bawling as if trying to say "thank you."

Chapter Twenty Seven

Sandy Gets Lost

Indian summer. A time when golden sunlight blends with the yellows and orange of poplar leaves that will soon come spinning down to earth. A time when the fiery reds of saskatoon, chokecherry and rose bush give a frivolous air to stolid brown hillsides rising lazily towards a powder-puff sky.

Circling the sloughs grizzled old willows with diamonds embedded deep beneath their warty bark, lean to admire the too-brief splendor of their bronze and ocher-tinted leaves. Curtseying and dimpling in the fairy breeze they laugh at their own reflection mirrored in the unrippled surface of the water.

The first good wind would bring coloured leaves whirling down to carpet the ground. Here, gently rustling and fluttering, or swirling, leaping, tumbling, goaded by the whim of every vagrant breeze, they perfume the air a while before sinking lower and lower until they themselves become a part of the soil, giving their richness for another season's growth.

The mosquitoes and horseflies are gone. The incessant, irritating hum of insects is replaced with the excited cawing of a hundred crows . . . they have found an uncut field of oats and are calling all their friends to come and feast with them.

Blackbirds, turning telephone wires into thick black rope, sway and twitter in the sunlight before flying off in a cloud to look for grain dropped in the stubble. Bluebirds, the same colour as the sky, flit from post to post, while meadow larks follow in a more leisurely fashion. Soon now they would all leave us.

At night the sky sparkles with a million stars. To stand quietly and listen is to hear the rush of many wings, the nostalgic, half-sad half-lonely call of the Canada Goose. While high in the northern sky the aurora borealis, a kaleidoscope of colour, dance and sway and crackle across the heavens like stately figures waltzing to mystic music.

The heady smells of combined straw, turning leaves and dry grass fill the air. It is an Alberta autumn in all its glory.

With the fall rush over it seemed like a good time to build an addition to the musk-ox paddock. Not that Sandy needed it, but Clarence was confident that somehow, somewhere, we would get another musk oxen and he wanted to be ready for her.

L. to R. Clarence Burpee, Jim Colp and Skinny Fisher, at lunch, while fencing

Now too was the time to build a new musk-ox barn to replace the old granary . . . one that someday could house individual pens for newly-weaned calves, as well as a stock-scale and a squeeze.

It looked an imposing structure for one little bull. Sandy thought so too and watched its construction with something more than casual interest. In fact he seemed to regard the project as his own. After watching the men pound nails he'd pick up the spare hammer in his mouth and walk around as if hoping to pound a few nails himself.

Nails? When Sandy found a bag of them there was invariably trouble. He'd shake the bag until it ripped, spilling nails in every direction or he'd push it around until the nails fell out. Either way was disaster.

The electric-saw fascinated him. Especially the cord. He'd unplug it then look surprised because the noise had stopped.

He got to be such a nuisance the men had to put their tools up on a work bench. That didn't stop Sandy. He'd jump onto the bench and continue being a nuisance. When chased away he'd look indignant. But he'd soon be back.

About this time Sandy developed a habit I didn't like. Clarence said he was just being friendly. I didn't see it that way. When my husband went into the musk-ox pasture the bull would run up and shove his head into Clarence's midriff. It might be a show of affection now, but it could easily become dangerous. What if the bull got rough and landed a good solid bunt?

Clarence scoffed at my fears and reminded me of the young bulls at College, Alaska who would frolic up to a man, shove their head tight against him and wait to be petted. I reminded him of a man in Norway who had been killed by a supposedly friendly musk ox.

But I had to admit Sandy did seem only to want attention.

When a metal cattle-squeeze was installed in the new musk-ox barn Sandy was curious. He'd sniff and chew experimentally on the iron bars. If the end-gate was up he'd step inside even if the front gate was shut and the only way out was back. Obviously he didn't realize how easily he could become trapped, for the first time Clarence let the end-gate shut on him it took him completely by surprise.

He got down on his knees to see if he could crawl out underneath. He stood anxiously on his hind legs to try and clamber out over the top. He tried pushing on the head-gate. When he finally realized he was a prisoner he became upset and gave off what Clarence calls his frightened smell. This is an acrid, pungent smell that while not entirely unpleasant, stings the nostrils. We had never noticed this odour around Musky when she first came to Gango Ranch and was in constant terror, so perhaps only bulls give off this scent.

Mention has often been made of a distinctive bull-smell during the rut. To our knowledge no one has ever spoken of a frightened smell, which in Sandy's case was readily noticeable whenever he was scared. Could this be a peculiarity not shared by all bulls? The smell served the purpose of telling us when Sandy was truly scared and not just putting on an act. So now Clarence quickly raised the end-gate and let him back to freedom.

Once he was safely out the bull stood as if trying to make up his mind. Was he scared enough to gallop away? Or . . . ? Finally he rolled his eyes heavenward as if calling on the spirit of some long-departed ancestor to be his witness and deliberately walked back into the squeeze again. He stood there just long enough to satisfy his ego, then backed out, a satisfied look on his face.

The next day Clarence had both end-gate and head-gate shut when Sandy came along and wanted in. No one paid any attention to him so he started snooping around. He soon discovered there was enough space under the tail-gate for his nose, and that when he raised it the gate moved.

In a few seconds he had the gate pried high enough so he could squeeze under it. Once inside, the gate dropped down behind him. But Sandy, like a dapper con-man who has pulled off a slick deal in sight of the police barracks, was too elated to notice he was trapped. He was so swelled up with pride and importance one almost expected him to pop like an over-blown balloon.

Sandy might not be worried, but Clarence was. If the musk ox pulled that trick when no one was around he could find himself shut in the squeeze for hours and become so excited and frightened he would hurt himself trying to get out.

To prevent this from happening Clarence wired the end-gate so he couldn't raise it. Sandy watching with a puzzled look on his shaggy face was probably wondering why somebody always had to spoil his fun.

* * *

Early in November Alberta's Indian Summer was whirled away on a snow storm. It was accompanied by plunging temperatures that made ranchers shake their heads and speculate. This might be another winter like 1919 . . . long and cold and hard, with cattle dying like poisoned flies. Some eyed their feed reserves nervously, then culled with a heavy hand.

One afternoon when there was no grass left showing above the snow, Clarence decided to let Sandy follow him out of the paddock. The bull meandered along behind, stopping often to investigate anything that caught his eye.

Then he'd hurry to catch up and snatch a mouthful of oats from the dish in my husband's hand. In this manner Sandy was led across the yard and down a long lane that ended at the stock-scale.

Sandy didn't hesitate about walking up onto the scales, then calmly watched while Clarence read the weigh-beam. Stockmen familiar with the way calves often panic when they hear the clang of metal and feel the scales sway beneath their feet will appreciate Sandy's unexpected behavior.

The musk ox wasn't frightened. He was too interested in the queer little knobs (weights on the weigh beam) that Clarence kept touching and looking at. Last February's teddy-bear-size musk oxen had grown into an impressive three-hundred-and-forty pounds of bull by November. It wasn't a spectacular gain, but Clarence was pleased.

Recently weaned Brown Swiss heifers, bug-eyed with curiosity, lined the fence bordering the weigh scales. They were fascinated by this hairy critter so different from the sleek animals they were used to.

Sandy, flattered by their attention, seemed to swell with importance as he looked them over. Then perhaps because he had more than a nodding acquaintance with mischief he gave a sharp snort that sent the heifers scuttling across the corral like scared jack rabbits.

Seeing that he looked at Clarence as if to say, "How about that? They're scared of me." The next moment his bawl was pleading with them to come back.

When he had them lined up, reaching out tentative noses to sniff him again he let go another snappy snort. One could almost hear him chuckle like a mischievous elf as they scampered away, bumping and jostling each other in their haste.

Then he looked at the fence and gave it a tentative push. If only it wasn't there. Playing with them could be such fun.

Clarence had to do a lot of coaxing to get Sandy to leave. Without the fence it would have taken more than grain to lure him away from the heifers.

His interest in the Brown Swiss youngsters seemed similar to Dr. Bernhard Grzimek's account of musk oxen released in Southern Norway earlier in the century.

Those animals got scattered and some of the bulls eventually turned up among domestic cattle in Sundalon. They began following the cows into the sheds at night and as long as no one tried to corner them appeared quite docile.

Not long after Sandy was weighed the men had to tattoo some pure-bred cattle and they wanted to use the squeeze in the musk-ox barn for the job. Sandy was moved to Image's temporarily empty corral so the heifers could be brought to the squeeze via the musk-ox paddock. Sandy didn't pay any attention to the cattle invading his premises. Perhaps because as long-yearlings they were too big to interest him.

However, he was interested in exploring the stallion paddock and he didn't miss a thing. He found a tiny space between the gate-post and the barn just big enough so that if he squeezed, wriggled and seriously put his mind to it, he could squirm through.

I was unsaddling Khem after bringing in the heifers when I saw Sandy casually sauntering around the yard with a look of pious innocence on his face. "Hey, Clarence! Your musk ox is out!" I yelled before hurrying to the house where a batch of bread was waiting to be baked.

The men waited to finish the heifer they were tattooing. It only took a minute, but in that minute Sandy disappeared.

When Clarence went to put him back the yard was empty. Sandy had vanished. My husband's face was bleak as if a hail storm had just wiped us out.

I ran to re-saddle Khem. The bread would have to wait. Rod was heading for the plane. It's easier to spot a critter from the air. Clarence was hurrying for the pick-up when a noise in the work-shop made him stop and turn. It sounded as if someone, something, had just upset a keg of nails.

The next moment Sandy poked his head out from between the work-shop doors, no doubt wondering what everyone was getting so steamed up about. He'd been having a good time poking his nose into a lot of things that shouldn't have concerned a musk ox, but now he was ready to follow his 'boss-man' back to the paddock.

Chapter Twenty Eight

School-Time

Clarence began breaking Sandy to lead on December 13th. It was no trouble to slip a halter on his head, but his heavy mane plus the fact he kept shaking his head to rid himself of the halter, made it hard to buckle the throat-strap. So Clarence replaced the halter with a lariat rope around Sandy's neck . Then he let him out into the barn.

When the bull realized he was caught he made a couple of crow-hops which would be considered tame by anyone who has taught foals to lead. After that Sandy pulled back a little and shook his head, but when the rope didn't shake off he was soon following his boss-man around the barn.

The next day when Sandy saw the halter in Clarence's hand he kept his nose pressed firmly into the oat dish. However, eventually he lifted his head and stood for the nose-band to be adjusted and the throat-latch fastened.

Sandy showed none of Musky's terror at being led. Within a couple of days he was leading so well Clarence brought him to the house to show me his progress. When leaving his paddock the bull fairly pulled the man in his haste to get going, but when returning he lagged like a five-year-old child thinking up excuses to delay going to bed.

Sandy looked forward to his walks with such anticipation Clarence had only to step inside the paddock and the bull was beside him sticking his head into the halter.

Sometimes they waded together through drifts in a poplar bluff. Even in the dead of winter Sandy found their twigs tasty, but he surprised us still more by stripping needles from pine boughs as if he thought them quite special.

Sandy follows Clarence

When Clarence cleared snow from the driveway it was piled up into huge pyramid mounds that froze and became rock hard. Sandy liked to scramble up them but he wanted to be first to the top. However, if Clarence beat him to the summit he would politely wait half way up until the man stepped down. Then it was his turn.

Outwardly Sandy was a halter-broke musk oxen, an animal that could be easily led anywhere, even places guaranteed to bring a balky glint into the eyes of the best-trained saddle horse.

Sandy, the King of the Castle

Clarence leaned a rough-hewn eighteen-inch plank up against the back of the three-ton farm truck as a ramp. When he walked up it Sandy was right behind him, sometimes in such a hurry he almost brushed Clarence off. Sandy found going up the ramp so simple that Clarence tried something else. He backed two half-ton trucks to within ten feet of each other, and used the plank to bridge the gap. Then he led Sandy across it. The musk ox crossed, turned and re-crossed as readily as a milk cow walks into her own stall.

Sandy would have tried climbing the outside stairs to the hayloft except Clarence was afraid if his foot slipped through a back opening he could get hurt. But he did hope the musk ox might climb with him to the top of a steep straw stack. Sandy tried, but the straw was too slippery. It kept sliding away.

Leading up a ramp

There is a two-wheeled pony cart on the ranch the kids called their freight wagon. It was just right for them to haul grass clippings away from the lawn or bring a couple of bags of potatoes in from the garden. It was used a lot when our children were Shetland-pony-age. Since then it has sat idle in a little-used corner of the yard. The day Sandy saw it he thought it looked worth investigating.

The box balances on the axle, so to keep it balanced it's important to distribute the load evenly. When Sandy started to step up into the box the weight of his front feet made the back-end hit the ground with a bump, while the front-end shot up into the air. Most animals would have been startled into bounding away as if from a two-headed demon. Not Sandy. He stepped the rest of the way in. Then stood teetering back and forth trying to get his weight evenly distributed. When he got the box balanced on its axle he looked so pleased with himself I almost expected him to take a bow.

He backed out the way he had come in, sending the front end shooting up into the air, but he didn't hurry or show any nervousness. One couldn't help but compare him to the jittery performance horses one sometimes sees being urged and cajoled by their riders, yet still refusing to cross a see-saw bridge in competitive trail classes.

When guests at our house asked to see Sandy my husband would quickly say "I'll bring him to the door so you won't need to go out in the cold." He wasn't just being kind. Or thoughtful. He enjoyed seeing their surprised reaction to a halter-broke musk oxen. When he opened the door to call "Sandy's here," Sandy didn't see any reason why he shouldn't come right on in. Sometimes he did manage to brush past Clarence and then his hooves left great dollops of snow on the floor. Reason enough for any housewife to decree "No musk oxen in this house."

Sandy was such a willing pupil Clarence began wondering if he could be taught to drive. This is not such a wild flight of fancy as it might first sound.

Both moose and reindeer have been successfully trained to pull sleds and carry a rider. In Russia where elk have been used as draft animals it is claimed a male weighing half-a-ton will pull loads three times his own weight. And there are documented instances of Russian noblemen using castrated stags to pull their carriages. Indeed an impressive sight if the animals carried a crown of antlers. And they probably did for authorities claim stags castrated while carrying a full set of horns won't shed, while those neutered before their antlers have grown are incapable of growing more. If that is indeed true then it seems likely elk driven by egocentric aristocrats had impressive racks of horns.

Refused admission to the house Sandy settles for a sprig from a rose-bush.

Despite success claimed with other game animals, we had never heard of anyone attempting to drive a musk ox. However there are reports of children riding musk oxen at Fort Chimo in Northern Quebec.

One day Clarence had sat momentarily on Sandy's back and while he was uneasy he hadn't panicked, or tried to run away. My husband, too heavy for our musk oxen's immature bones and tendons, had only wanted to see what Sandy would do. Not ride him. Teaching the bull to drive was another matter.

For the first lesson Clarence snapped a long rope to the halter and walked behind Sandy. The musk ox quickly learned to respond, turning each time he felt a pull on the halter. However, with only one rope, his turns, of necessity, were all in the same direction.

The next day Clarence used two long ropes, one on either side. That upset Sandy. He became scared and tried to run away, giving off his frightened smell, Something about seeing a rope on either side made him feel trapped.

Some young horses feel the same way the first time they are driven. We have found they respond more readily to their first driving lesson if they have previously been worked on a longe line. This not only teaches them the commands "get-up" and "whoa", "walk" and "trot", but it is good preparation for further training. Clarence decided to try Sandy on a longe-line.

For a musk ox Sandy did well the first lesson. He learned that when tapped on the rump he was to go forward. And that is progress indeed for an animal who instinctively turns to attack anything touching its hind-end.

However, Sandy found it hard to understand why he should walk around Clarence when he would much rather walk up to him. Although he would move forward on command he'd stop every few feet to see if his boss-man didn't think this nonsense had gone far enough. When Clarence insisted he must go on, he plodded through the snow, grunting complaints at every step and looking very down-trodden.

After working Sandy on the longe line for a few minutes each day for a week, Clarence tried driving him again. This time he had a helper. With two people, neither of whom walked directly behind him, the animal went much better.

However, when Clarence took both ropes and tried driving him without help Sandy would circle him, preferably on the run, but he didn't want anyone holding two ropes walking behind him.

This made us realize it would take a lot of training to teach Sandy to drive, and he'd never tolerate a cart, so Clarence gave up the driving lessons.

One day when a wild wind was blasting the land Clarence threw a big sheet of black plastic down in front of Sandy and stood on one corner so it couldn't leave the country.

Flapping, snapping, pulsating, billowing up as if it were something alive, it was enough to scare most animals. But Sandy ran up and jumped on it. When the wind sent it surging up around him he playfully bunted it back down. He looked as pleased as a king with a new crown each time he drove the air out from under it and it sank back, rustling and sighing to writhe and twitch restlessly on the ground until another gust of wind swept under it.

* * *

Ever since Sandy had learned to lead, Clarence had been taking him to the weigh scales once a week to be weighed. We were disappointed he wasn't gaining more. However, we knew it is not unusual for some wild animals to go into semi-hibernation in winter, the season when food is normally scarce. Their metabolism slows down and they eat less. This trait carries over into well-fed herds. We knew the pampered musk oxen at Fairbanks make no noticeable weight-gains for a period of two or three months in mid-winter.

Still, we wondered if internal parasites might be slowing Sandy's growth, so in February we sent away a specimen of his faeces for testing. It showed traces of a roundworm, a coccidia parasite found in cattle, goats and sheep. He would have to be de-wormed.

This time the prescribed treatment was a Ripercol bolus. Clarence crushed it into a powder and mixed it with grain but Sandy detected it almost immediately and managed to eat the oats, leaving the medicine in the feed box.

Clarence decided he would have to give Sandy a bolus with a balling-gun.

"How's he going to shove a balling-gun down that critter's throat?" I wondered. Horses often object rather strenuously to the same treatment, and I supposed a musk ox would be even harder to treat, but I didn't voice my fears. Clarence doesn't appreciate my gloomy prophesies.

Actually it was no trouble at all.

He began by feeding Sandy horse crunchies, (pellets the same size as the bolus), first from his fingers, then from the balling gun. After a half dozen or so crunchies he loaded the gun with the bolus, stuck his fingers in the side of Sandy's mouth and while the animal was trying to sort through fingers with his tongue to find the crunchy, pushed the gun down his gullet and expelled the medicne. Sandy was still looking for the crunchy when the bolus was well on its way to his stomach.

Now that Sandy was so quiet and easy to handle collecting his qiviut in the spring shouldn't be a problem. The previous year he had been nervous and his wool so thin and scraggly we hadn't bothered with it. This year was different. Sandy was as friendly as a pet pig. He had a fine thick undercoat. He had complete trust in Clarence. No need for gloomy premonitions.

Sandy poses for his picture.

Chapter Twenty Nine

Near Escape

Spring calving, followed by the dawn-to-dark rush to get the crop in, cut drastically into the time Clarence had to spend with Sandy. If the musk ox felt neglected it didn't show. Not until May when he started to shed. Then he developed a Dr. Jekyll-Mr. Hyde personality.

The first indication of this was the evening Clarence picked off a gob of qiviut dangling loosely from the Sandy's shoulder. The bull snorted and backed away. Clarence not knowing what he had done to startle the musk ox, called him back.

This time when my husband reached for more of the qiviut giving Sandy's coat a down-on-one's-luck shabbiness, his eyes rolled in near panic. He gave a wild, peremptory snort and ran stamping to the far side of the paddock. Yet when he came back and Clarence showed him the handful of qiviut he sniffed it as he might any object of no special interest to him. It seemed that it was watching the hand removing his qiviut that he found upsetting. No one was going to pull out this musk oxen's stuffing.

In the days that followed, as more qiviut began working out through the guard hairs, Sandy became progressively harder to handle.

His animosity towards the squeeze grew out of all proportion, especially when one remembered the fascination it had held for him such a short time before. He avoided it now with the dedication of picnickers avoiding a grizzly with cubs.

The sight of a rope would send him stamping to the far

side of the paddock. When Clarence did manage to halter him he fought like a wild mustang. What had happened to our halter-broke musk oxen?

Clarence discovered the best way to gather qiviut was to cover Sandy's near eye. When he couldn't see the hand reaching for the hanks of qiviut dangling from his body, he stood quietly.

My husband supposed Sandy's personality switch must be due to a hormone imbalance brought on by the shedding process. It seemed to have some similarity to the behavioral change in bulls during the rut. He didn't expect it to last.

By late July Sandy appeared to be over his antagonism towards a rope so Clarence decided to lead him to the weigh scales. As a precaution he took along an oat dish. Sandy always followed for oats.

The bull led nicely until he reached the holding-pen near the scales. Then his Mr. Hyde personality came swirling back. His eyes had the dangerous glitter of a disturbed rattlesnake. He charged the oat dish and sent it spinning. Before Clarence had recovered from that surprise he galloped away, jerking the rope from the man's hands.

My husband was able to retrieve the long, trailing lasso and this time he braced himself, so if Sandy ran off again he could hold him. The bull immediately hit the end of the rope with a jolt that jerked him end for end. Yet in spite of that, or perhaps because of it, he went on a charging binge that must have given him a sore neck. It certainly did nothing to improve his humour.

After a battle that would have made wild-horse-wrestling dull by comparison Sandy was shut in the chute leading to the scales.

Believing the animal would be safe enough there for a few minutes, Clarence dropped the rope and went to adjust the weigh-beam. He expected the musk ox to either follow, or stand puffing and panting until he came back. But Sandy had on a high head of steam. He did neither.

He tried to climb over the seven-foot fence separating him from Khem.

The stallion, tail arched high , red mane whipping, was dancing angrily up and down, snorting and rearing, hooves pawing empty air. His blazing eyes, wide-flaring nostrils, ears alternatively pricked in interest, then laid flat back in anger were giving a clear warning he would tolerate no invasion of his domain.

Sandy, not understanding stallion language, ignored the warning.

When he found the fence too high to climb over he got down on his knees and pushed his head under the bottom plank. A little wiggle, a squirm, a shove and he'd be in with the stallion.

Khem had once killed a calf that had been foolish enough to squeeze its way into his corral. What if he did the same with Sandy?

I screamed at Khem. He was too excited to pay any attention. So I screamed at Clarence. What was taking him so ungodly long. "Hurry Up!" I shrieked. "Sandy'll be killed!"

That brought Sandy back up on his feet. He went crashing down the chute and slithered onto the scales.

When he found himself trapped he reared and tried to turn, and in the process got one foot jammed between the iron railings.

"Oh Lord! Now he'll break a leg." I wished I'd never heard of musk oxen.

However, as quickly as the end-gate was raised he jerked his foot loose and went crashing back up the chute ricocheting from side to side, the trailing rope burning the wind.

Clarence went after him and in a few minutes had the end of the lariat. But he couldn't lead Sandy. Without giving the rope a couple of quick wraps around a post he couldn't even hold him.

Eventually by snubbing the rope first around one post, then another, we had worked Sandy to within a few feet of his own paddock. But with our musk ox fighting like a crazed buffalo those few feet loomed as a challenging eternity of time and distance. We had run out of posts to snub to.

If Sandy got away now he could run for miles. And he seemed to realize this. I ran to grab the end of the lasso to try and help Clarence hold him.

Swirling around in great black pools of fury Sandy slammed into the end of the rope with a jolt that threw him heavily to the ground. He landed with a hard thud. And lay still. My throat went dry. I'd seen a horse kill itself that way.

Clarence's face was drenched in sweat. There was a taut expression around his mouth, the veins stood out purple on his forehead, his knuckles showed white where they gripped the rope.

Shocked and numb we waited . . . watched . . . for an eternity . . . for a minute . . . perhaps it was only a fleeting moment of time, a moment that with its passing brought a tremor, an almost invisible shudder to the body before us.

Slowly Sandy stirred, then hoisted himself up from the ground. As he did he shook himself and glared at Clarence.

His eyes glittered with crafty intent as he began deliberately backing away from the rope, his head tilted so the noose would slip forward over one ear.

I leaped forward as if electrified, yelling, "Slacken the rope! It's coming off!"

Even as I ran, intending to drive him ahead to give Clarence the chance he needed to work the rope back into place, the musk ox flipped his head. The rope slid off over the other ear and dropped to the ground.

Was the look on Sandy's face surprise? Or smug satisfaction? He turned and raced down the hill like a greyhound sprung from a starting gate.

"How are we going to get him back?" Clarence didn't answer. Because he didn't know. He looked like a paratrooper who has suddenly realized his parachute isn't going to open.

The Arabian mares weren't far away. If Sandy tried to make friends with them I could call them and they would come. But would he follow them back? What if the mares, always protective of their foals, took off when they saw a musk ox in their midst? What if in their wild flight some of them ran smack into a barbed wire fence? Bubbles of fear began percolating deep within me as a vision of mangled horse-flesh invaded my brain.

We had to act quickly, but I wasn't sure how.

Should I saddle Khem? He handles ornery cows like an old pro, but a musk ox might be something else.

If Sandy charged him what would the stallion do? He comes from a line of Arabians bred by Egyptian princes for their bravery under attack. If Khem followed his primal instincts and fought the musk ox could I stop him? For that matter could I stay on him? I wasn't sure.

All these thoughts flashed with lightning speed through my mind as Clarence raced past with long, loping strides, rope in hand, intending to try and head Sandy off.

"What a hope!" I groaned and reluctantly turned to get Khem. There didn't seem any other alternative.

But before I got to Khem I saw the oat-dish discarded where Sandy had bunted it. Surprisingly there was till some grain in it. Something made me pick it up and walk back towards Sandy who had stopped and was watching Clarence suspiciously. "Come Sandy" I called, shaking the oats. The musk ox looked towards me, then back to Clarence. He licked his lips. I shook the oats again. He took a step forward. I took one towards him, shaking the oats. He started walking slowly towards me. As he came he kept looking back to make sure the man with the rope wasn't attempting to sneak up on him.

Soon Sandy, still keeping a wary eye on Clarence, was eating from the dish in my hand.

Turning I walked slowly towards the musk-ox paddock, holding the dish behind me so he could eat as he followed. I hoped the oats held out. I hoped with even greater fervency that he wouldn't charge the dish again. If he did I'd be worm feed. Trying to keep fear from showing in my voice I encouraged Sandy (and myself) with a steady stream of chatter. If he became frightened or suspicious and ran away now, the day was lost. My heart sounded louder than African tom-toms when I reached the gateway and walked through it. Sandy followed.

He was inside now, but I had to get back to the gate and shut it, without arousing his suspicions. Still talking I moved well into the paddock, set the dish down, and while he was contentedly munching grain eased around him and back to the gate.

My adrenaline was pumping furiously as I shoved the gate shut just as Clarence reached it. The strained look had gone from his eyes. Now the grin playing about the corners of his mouth lit his face like the eternal flame.

"Can you beat that?" I exclaimed sagging on knees that suddenly felt as if they were made of warm jello. I wiped streaks of sweat from my forehead with a dirty hand as my husband quietly coiled the musk-ox rope and hung it on a peg beside the outgrown halter. They could gather dust together.

Kivy, the New Heifer

Winter had once more plunged the land into a deep-freeze when I looked out my kitchen window and saw Sandy plodding along behind Clarence like an old school pony. The rope around his neck was slack, and it stayed slack as he followed the man up a plank and into the three-ton truck. That could only mean our musk oxen was leading again, just as he had done last winter.

At an igloo on Gango Ranch

That started us wondering. Does the musk-ox personality change with the seasons? Perhaps.

An oil man once told us he had walked up to a lone musk-ox cow on one of the high Arctic Island in the dead of winter and petted her before she stamped away. He said it was because she was stupid with cold.

"Cold? A musk ox cold?" But he had only shaken his head. There didn't seem any other explanation.

Clarence was taking Sandy on daily walks again when he got word of a six-month-old heifer available at the Alberta Game Farm. Did he want her?

Does a miser want gold?

But I nearly choked when I heard the price. One could build a modern bungalow for that. Our two-story sixty-year old home with its sweeping veranda and hand-carved gingerbreads was outdated but I suddenly realized I didn't want a new house. This one had personality and character. It was full of memories. Mostly happy. It had become a part of me. So plans were made to get the heifer in January, but before we did we wanted her insured. Lloyds of London would insure musk oxen at what we thought was quite a reasonable premium.

Musky's terror and subsequent trauma at being crated made Clarence want to try something different when he went for the heifer. As he watched Sandy contentedly chewing his cud, he pulled off a mitt, thoughtfully held his hand over a cold spot on one cheek and soliloquized: "If I take Sandy with me when I go for the heifer she shouldn't find the trip home so scary."

"But what about Sandy?" I objected, "He would have to go both ways?"

"He won't mind." To prove his point Clarence started taking Sandy on short truck rides around the ranch. Sandy got quite used to it and seemed to feel his new role as travelling musk ox was rather an important one.

For the 150-mile trip to the Alberta Game Farm the truck box, tarped and bedded with straw, had a forkful of alfalfa hay thrown in. It would be an all-day trip and Sandy might like to snack. However, he spent most of the three-hour drive to the Game Farm lying down chewing his cud. We had a peek-hole so we could see him from the cab.

A wave of apprehension hit me when I saw the heifer. She looked dreadfully tiny and she had a dirty behind. I asked if she had scours and didn't get an answer. However, the Game Farm veterinarian checked her out as healthy, the insurance went into effect, and I breathed easier.

Meanwhile Sandy was causing a stir. The Game Farm staff weren't used to seeing a big musk-ox bull calmly watch them through the slatted end-gate of a truck. They were more familiar with bulls who put people over fences and smashed up trucks.

Clarence planned to fasten Sandy to the front of the truck-box before the heifer was caught. He anticipated enough trouble getting her loaded without the bull getting in the way at the wrong time.

As he stepped up into the truck there were hasty whispers and furtive remarks. The farm workers found it hard to believe anyone would be stupid enough to become a willing target for a musk ox . . . even if the animal was supposed to be tame. They were laying odds as to the outcome.

They seemed unnecessarily disappointed, I thought, when nothing happened.

Now it was time to catch Kivy, our new heifer.

Six husky men, with the physique of professional football players, were grouped around the door into the pen. They looked edgy as they shifted about uneasily. Their wise-cracking about hospital insurance and funeral costs had grim undertones. However, they were all prepared to surge through the door the moment their leader gave the signal.

Several people wanting to watch (me among them) climbed onto a nearby pile of bales to get an unobstructed view.

As the men burst through the door, fanning out to surround the musk ox there was sheer panic in her eyes. Hoping to escape them she hurled herself into the air as if she was an arrow launched at me. Instinctively I stepped back, stumbled, lurched and half fell off the bales. A convenient pair of arms saved me from a nasty fall. I shot the man a self conscious "thank you" and climbed right back up again. I didn't want to miss anything .

I was in time to see a beautifully synchronized capture. One man dove and had the heifer around the neck in an amorous embrace, a second pair of arms were hugging her middle, this man's face buried in the long hair on her shoulder. At the same moment each of her legs miraculously sprouted a man.

The heifer, frantic to escape snorted and bawled, twisted and squirmed but it was six against one.

Before the men carried her to the waiting truck Clarence put in an ear tag, (the type stockmen use for cattle) identifying her with name and number. He said afterwards getting the tag into her ear was like trying to punch a hole in the hide of a tough old Hereford bull. Musk oxen have a much thicker hide than cattle.

As the men hoisted Kivy up into the truck they shoved her towards Sandy and slammed the end-gate shut. Sandy had a look of blank astonishment on his face. Where had she come from?

When Clarence reached through from the outside to untie the bull he sniffed at her, then feinted a bunt. She stepped away with the calm that precedes a hail storm.

Sandy just snorted. He was telling her he was boss and would tolerate no nonsense. She evidently understood for they rode home so quietly that we stopped several times to convince ourselves we still had two musk oxen.

When Clarence backed the truck up to the unloading chute I sat on the top rail of the paddock and watched. Many thoughts flashed through my mind.

Musky was gone. . . . the end of that dream. But she had taught us much we needed to know if other dreams were to reach fruition. Now we knew even the wildest musk-ox calf will, with time and patience, learn to trust humans. There didn't seem any reason to suppose we couldn't tame Kivy. But what about domestication?

Watching the two musk oxen run down the unloading chute and across the paddock I remembered reading the findings of the 1919 Royal Commission on the feasibility of domesticating musk ox . "The conservation and domestication of the musk ox are matters of great domestic importance. There is apparently no question as to the musk-ox adaptability to domestication, and if the matter is gone about in an intelligent and business like way, any expenditure which may be incurred will be amply repaid."

That report came out many years ago and still there was no Government involvement. We were in this thing on our own.

I sighed, climbed down off the fence and walked hand in hand with Clarence to the house.

Chapter Thirty One

Vet Clinic Makes History

Taming Kivy was made easier by her habit of running to Sandy when frightened. Clarence could then reach across the bull's back and touch her. At first she'd jump as if hit with an electric shock and run off, but when Sandy wouldn't follow she'd soon come back.

Before long she learned hands didn't hurt, and that they often held a treat. After that Sandy could move without her flying into a panic.

Eventually Clarence was able to rub his hand down her shoulder, and leg, even ask for a foot and she would often give it. In time he could reach under her belly and feel the undeveloped teats hidden beneath a dense coat of hair . . . an accomplishment that would prove of value at a later date.

By the time Spring came Clarence had no trouble combing qiviut from Kivy while she was loose in the corral. Whereas Sandy, quieter in every other respect, had to be put in the chute before his qiviut could be touched.

In mid-summer Clarence decided to truck the musk oxen to 160 acres of grass and bush land he had fenced for them. Immediately I protested. "What if something happens and you have to bring them home before you get the lane fenced?" It could be months before we got that finished.

Clarence shrugged as if that possibility was of no importance.

Two Arabian fillies had been the sole occupants of the link-wire sanctuary. Now we wondered how they would re-act to sharing it with musk oxen.

The fillies looked surprised when Sandy and Kivy walked down the unloading ramp. But that didn't prevent them from coming up to us to be petted. As soon as we drove off musk oxen and horses sniffed noses. Magic, the gray filly, the older of the two, wheeled, considering the advisability of kicking, but Kivy gave a snort, accompanied by a threatening stamp and both horses scampered away.

From then on horses and musk oxen always pastured within sight of each other. Occasionally Sandy would snort and streak towards them in a stiff-legged humping run. When that happened the fillies galloped away, but as soon as he stopped they stopped too and began grazing again.

Horses and musk oxen happily together

Sandy charged after Kivy in the same way, often chasing her all around the pasture. Then they'd both stop and begin eating as if nothing unusual had happened. Sometimes Kivy would mince up to Sandy playfully shaking her head, inviting, (or maybe daring) him to charge. This happened more often as the rut approached.

Before the musk oxen had been in their new pasture for a month we had reason to wish they were still in their home paddock.

* * *

It wasn't the drenching rain that brings smiles to farmers' faces, but only a half-hearted drizzle that did little except stop haying. It was on such a day that Clarence drove out to see the musk oxen. He wasn't surprised to see their coats bedraggled. The hair on their foreheads, sodden from browsing among tall grass and moisture-laden bushes, was plastered tight to their skulls giving them a drowned rat appearance, It was this that alerted Clarence. Something about Sandy didn't look right. A closer inspection told him the bull had a raw sore around one horn. The horn, because the original dehorning operation hadn't been satisfactory for a musk ox, was growing back deformed. It was now gouging into his head. It looked serious.

Clarence's face was grave when he returned to the house saying "I'll have to take Sandy to the Clinic."

That brought rocks to my stomach.

"Take Sandy to the Clinic! What's the matter? Couldn't the vet come down?" the questions tumbled out."

Weariness, and worry, had brought lines of fatigue around my husband's eyes. "I can't tell how deeply the horn is embedded in his skull. It looks bad. There could be complications. If there are, the vet would be better able to handle them at the Clinic."

"Complications?" I gulped. My husband, the optimist in our family, the one who never looks for trouble, was more worried than I'd seen him for a long time. Was it already too late for Sandy? My mind skipped like a flat stone on water back to Musky. Her death.

Weakness trickled through me. I had to sit down.

While Clarence was phoning the vet I stewed over perceived problems. The musk ox were in a pasture with a perimeter fence, and nothing else.

"Sandy won't lead." I reminded Clarence when he had hung up. "You know what happened a year ago."

"He probably won't follow either. Not if it means leaving Kivy." Clarence's words sounded jaded, as if they had run out of the steam.

The half-mile separating pasture from paddock stretched until it assumed Brobdingnagian proportions.

"Couldn't you take out a few gates and make a temporary corral?" My voice was hopeful.

"Probably. But it would take too long. Sandy has to be at the Clinic by 9 tomorrow morning." It was already late afternoon. "I'll take out the truck and loading chute. If Sandy isn't too sick he'll probably go into the truck out of curiosity."

"Then I better get you some corn stalks from the garden. That might help to coax him in. " Sandy loved corn almost as much as Musky had.

While Clarence readied the truck I got the corn, and in case that wasn't enough I fetched a mixture of oats and beet pellets too.

As soon as we were within sight of the musk ox Clarence stopped the truck and backed it up to the loading chute. Sandy wasn't paying any attention until Clarence called him and rustled the corn, then he moved towards us. As he did Clarence dropped a trail of corn stalks up the chute-ramp, and some inside the truck box too. Then he stepped back to watch. I stayed inside the cab. I never quite trusted Sandy. Not the way my husband did. The bull walked twice around chute and truck, then as if his curiosity was satisfied, he walked up the ramp and into the truck, eating corn as he went. As Clarence closed the end-gate I jumped out looking relieved. "That was easy."

So was re-loading Sandy again the next morning at the paddock. The truck was well tarped so the drive over to Wainwright should be routine too. It was when Sandy got to the veterinary Clinic that things might get out of hand.

The Clinic's pens and squeezes are designed for cattle and horses. Not musk oxen.

I'd had enough experience with gentle Arabians who went wild eyed and snorty when they found themselves surrounded by antiseptic smells, and strange surroundings, to have any illusions about Sandy.

I'd persuaded Clarence to stop and pick up Allan Currier. It wouldn't do any harm to have a man good with a rope along.

However, Clarence did look surprised when I opted to stay home, but he nodded his understanding at my explanation. "If there's trouble I'd rather not be there to see it."

That explanation satisfied my husband. It left me wondering at myself. I've always been one who wanted to be where the action was. Today I didn't. Was that an omen?

As the truck disappeared in a swirling cloud of grey dust I headed for the barn, intending to busy myself with the horses to keep from worrying. That usually works. It didn't today.

I knew Clarence was concerned about Sandy. Not so much about the actual cutting away of the misshapen horn and pulling it out of Sandy's head, as about the damage they would find beneath it.

The possibility that Sandy might cause a ruckus never seemed to have entered my husband's mind. It never left mine. I couldn't forget the memory of Musky rolling out dead at my feet. Or the docile beef bulls who panicked and broke out of the vet Clinic. There was no shortage of possible catastrophes to stew about.

Sandy unloaded well. He walked willingly into the squeeze where animals are restrained for veterinarian examination. His head appeared to be held securely enough when the vet started to probe the horn area. However, the probing hurt so Sandy shook his head as any animal might to drive off a bothersome fly.

It was only a little shake, but for whatever reason it loosened a key-pin in the head-gate and the whole squeeze quite literally fell apart.

Sandy stood a minute as if not quite sure what was expected of him, then walked into the "people" part of the building. Someone had the presence of mind to quickly yank down the overhead door and block the way outside. But without its safety catch, one little bunt would have sent the door flying up again.

Today there were more people than normal at the Vet Clinic. Word had got around that a musk ox was coming in. And for many that meant their first look at one of the mysterious, and somewhat mythical survivors of the last ice age.

Now Sandy was loose among those people. And like disturbed flies they shot up to sit atop the closest gate or highest partition. Then nervously looked to see if they could climb still higher should the musk ox move in their direction.

The vets watched grim eyed as Sandy walked among their x-ray equipment, past shelves of medicine, squeezed between surgical tables gleaming with an array of sterilized instruments ready to be moved quickly when needed to any operating theatre in the clinic.

Clarence looked as if he was holding a ticking bomb, and not quite sure what to do with it. If he caught Sandy, and the musk ox fought, as he might, the Clinic would look like the aftermath of a tornado. If he didn't, and Sandy accidentally upset a table or knocked over the medicine shelves, he might fly into a panic as destructive as a summer hail storm. Or if someone from the outside opened the door Sandy could be gone in a flash.

With a feeling that whatever he did might be a mistake Clarence walked quietly up to Sandy, slipped a rope over his head, and at the same time held out his free hand saying "Come on Sandy." Sandy, expecting a treat, followed his owner back into the animal part of the Clinic

"Well, I'll be gol durned!" rumbled one old rancher after emptying his mouth of a long-overdue squirt of tobacco juice. "There ain't another dad-blamed critter in this country that wouldn't have wrecked the place first."

It didn't take long to repair the squeeze and put Sandy back in it. This time everything held, and the horn was soon off. It hadn't done nearly the damage Clarence had feared. Daily dusting with an antibiotic powder for a few days and Sandy could go back out to rcjoin Kivy.

Chapter Thirty Two

Mating Time

The summer of 1976 Sandy developed a habit we didn't like. He began charging into the link-wire fence. At first he seemed to be playing, but if anyone chanced to be on the other side his playing turned dangerous.

I thought I could break him of the habit by switching him on the nose as I had done with Musky. However, I discovered it is all but impossible to hit anything when you have to poke the switch through a small opening in a link-wire fence. To make matters worse, when Sandy hit the wire it billowed out towards me like a wind-filled sail. I had to step back, or be hit. And that inflated his ego.

So I got a heavier stick intending to whack him over the head when he plowed into the wire. That was even less effective. Sandy thought I was challenging him to a fight, and he was all for that.

Now when he saw me he'd swagger towards me at a swaying rhythmic pace, faster than a walk, yet not quite a run, his head cocked to present-the-horn, his mane stiff and erect, his eyes flashing fire. He looked big and explosive. I didn't stay around to argue.

Should a car drive alongside the fence now he'd gallop beside it, keeping pace at an effortless gait we clocked at better than twenty-miles per hour. If the driver got too far ahead, or swung away, Sandy would stop and take out his frustrations on the fence.

We had to reinforce the link-wire, adding top and bottom tension wires, and a third at "charge" level. Even so a fence can only absorb so much punishment. As the paddock fence bordering the garden came in for the most abuse, Clarence put a guard rail of heavy-steel pipe mounted on equally sturdy steel posts along the inside of the paddock about eighteen inches back from the wire.

The first time Sandy saw the steel piping he plowed into it with the same reckless abandon he used on other fences. Only there was no give to this. It stopped him with a body jarring jolt.

I began to feel safe again when working in the garden alongside his paddock. Sandy would still fume up to the guard rail with blood in his eye. He'd snort and belch, tossing his head and pawing in frustration, but he never hit it again.

The sight of us now, even though half-a-mile away, affected him like a lodestone. He'd fling up his head and start towards us at a swinging pace which quickly changed into a frenzied gallop. His long hair whipped in the wind, which carried with it strange belching noises. At first we thought Sandy must have gas in astronomical amounts until we realized his deep belly burps were in fact menacing threats. He also developed an overpowering odour, which we know now is common to all breeding bulls. It becomes especially noticeable during the rut. (This could explain why northern explorers who encountered musk oxen in the autumn, named them as they did.)

Sandy's lust-crazed mind saw us, especially Clarence, as rivals. For days he was so insane with jealousy and the drive to dominate his territory he wouldn't take time to eat or sleep.

His eyes were red-ringed with hate, the peculiar male odour grew stronger and he became so moody and belligerent even Kivy tried to avoid him.

The morning of October 13th, 1976 both Sandy and Kivy seemed different. He was urgently nuzzling her neck and face, and she didn't seem to mind. This was a change from the passion inflamed dashes that for days had sent him streaking after Kivy, grunting love calls that only caused Kivy to put as much distance as possible between herself and their source.

The moment he saw anyone step outside the house he'd whirl from Kivy's side and rush up to the fence. We felt safer knowing he was in a paddock with iron guard-rails.

His mating urge, driven now to a white-hot seething boil, had put him in such a turmoil he could scarcely take time to mount Kivy before having to jump down to charge threateningly towards anything, real or imaginary, that moved. He even charged a butterfly fluttering on a nearby flower. Then he would rush back to Kivy and try to mount again.

Kivy wasn't always co-operative and although we saw him mount her three times in the course of the morning we weren't sure if he ever actually bred her. We didn't know if she wasn't quite in standing heat, or if Sandy was too excited to stay and finish the job.

That afternoon we had to leave for Saskatoon. When we got back two days later Sandy was much less aggressive, and by the end of the month he was almost his old self again.

Chapter Thirty Three

Kivy's Calf 'Esky'

As winter gave way to spring we kept a careful watch on Kivy. Was her belly swelling? Or was it only wishful thinking? Our hopes fluctuated like the temperature until finally a day came when we reluctantly acknowledged there would be no calf. Her figure was too trim.

Sandy got the blame. Perhaps he wasn't fertile. Had his earlier close association with humans affected his sexual drive? It can happen. And if it had would the problem reverse itself after another season with Kivy?

Clarence, always the optimist, hadn't completely written off the possibility of a calf. He kept saying "She hasn't started to shed yet."

He knew, as did I, that knowledgeable northerners claim musk ox cows won't shed until after calving. By the time most of Sandy's underwear had surfaced, and Kivy's coat still looked sleek and smooth, even my hopes began to rise.

Then came the day when they plummeted. Kivy was shedding. There would be no calf. Not this year.

However, we would soon have reason to hope again.

One sunny May morning when the meadow larks were singing from the fence posts and Clarence was taking qiviut from Kivy and stuffing it in his pocket, he ran a hand under her belly and back towards her teats.

She snorted and stepped away, but he tried again and thought he detected some slight swelling. A thrill surged over him but he was determined to be realistic. What he had felt might only be the normal mammary development of a maturing animal.

A few days later Clarence felt Kivy's teats again. This time he couldn't keep the excitement from his voice. "I'm sure she's in calf."

However, he has been a rancher too long to count profits before the sale. Or calves before they are born. What statistics there are claim the mortality rate among first-born musk-ox calves is high. Nearly half the calves born to musk-ox heifers are stillborn.

Another question started bothering us. What is the length of a musk oxen's gestation?

The only reports on that subject "believed" it to be eight months. Knowing how few people have seen the mating of musk oxen, or been present at the subsequent birth, it was easy to understand the lack of data. Besides, what if the "eight-month gestation" was in the same class as "pregnant cows don't shed"?

Before the first week in June had slipped into history Kivy was spending a lot of time walking anxiously up and down the fence separating her from Sandy. On June 9th, a day too hot even for mad dogs and Englishmen to be about, she frequently broke into a fast gallop, apparently oblivious to the heat.

That night Clarence put her in the home paddock where he could watch her more closely. In the morning I half expected to see her with a calf, but she was still walking.

However, near noon I had seen Kivy lie down twice, them immediately scramble to her feet again. She appeared uncomfortable. Clarence thought it could be hours before she went into real labour. So he went back out to finish cultivating. Kivy's eight months weren't up yet.

There was a funeral at two o'clock that afternoon which I felt obliged to go to. However as soon as decency would permit I did slip away. Then felt guilty for leaving so quickly when I drove into the yard and saw Kivy standing quietly in her paddock. There was no sign of a calf.

But wait. What was that? Wanting a better look I walked slowly closer. That brought an angry snort from Kivy. And she started rubbing her nose on a nearby stump. She had never accepted me as Musky had, but still . . . this animosity seemed a bit much. I backed quickly and went for the binoculars. There didn't seem any point in riling her unnecessarily. Even with the binoculars I couldn't be sure. But what I thought I saw was a small whitish balloon below her stub tail. Without waiting to verify it, I ran to the car and went for Clarence.

When we got back a few minutes later Kivy was walking again, the balloon was gone and in its place were two tiny dark hooves. Clarence ran to get the calf-pullers, more out of custom than because he had any serious thought he might be able to use them.

When Kivy saw me she became very agitated, working herself into such a frenzy I hid in tall grass where I could watch without her seeing me. Although she must have known I was there, she calmed down almost immediately. Was it out-of-sight, out-of-mind?

"Be careful. She's tigerish" I hissed as Clarence strode past. Instead of answering he let himself into her paddock.

Watching Kivy hurry with stiff, determined stride towards Clarence made my breath freeze. . . . Why was he still standing there? Why wasn't he climbing the fence? I'd have been long gone. Then the frozen air swooshed from my lungs in great chunks of astonishment. She wasn't attacking him, she was sniffing at his hands, his overalls, even his shoes; then she turned and headed back to the little clump of trees she had just left, stopping every few steps to look back to make sure he was still following. Great Thundering Guns! The animal actually seemed to be asking for his help.

As soon as she reached the trees she flopped to the ground and lay flat on her side. Her legs, sticking out like posts, jerked each time her powerful stomach muscles worked to force out the body waiting to be born. Clarence cautiously did a quick examination.

It seemed a normal enough presentation, but the feet looked limp. Lifeless.

Quickly, there was no time to loose . . . it might already be too late . . . he slipped the calf-chains over the tiny hooves, Now when Kivy strained he helped with a steady downward pressure on the chains.

In moments a little black head lying compactly between two front legs slid into sight. As it did Kivy sprang to her feet as if stung by a bee, and bounded across the paddock at a body-jarring gallop.

I watched too startled to breathe. If that calf wasn't already dead it would be now. What was the stupid critter trying to do? Shake it out?

The limp little body swinging lifelessly back and forth like a wet dish-rag was jolted further and further out, until it fell to the ground with a sodden plop. Instantly Kivy whirled and was at her calf's side. Clarence was there almost as soon, calling out excitedly, "It's alive! And it's a heifer!"

I felt like throwing my hat in the air and cheering. Instead I ran to the house for the camera.

Musk ox and man, heads almost touching, worked as a team to dry off the newborn calf. Kivy licked it with her rough tongue. Clarence rubbed it with handfulls of grass.

Each time either of them touched it the calf opened its mouth very wide, stuck out a cherry-red tongue and gave a loud, resentful blat.

For the first thirty minutes of its life the calf made no attempt to rise but used its energy to blat loud and often.

Compared to foals who are normally discovering their legs within minutes of birth, this calf's inactivity seemed unusual. I hoped there was nothing wrong.

Kivy's new calf 'Esky'

Clarence left the final drying-off to Kivy and came for the camera to take close-up pictures. When Kivy saw the camera she left her calf to investigate it thoroughly, sniffing the box, the lens, taking the carrying strap in her mouth and giving it a little tug. Then apparently satisfied she went back to her offspring. However, each time the camera clicked she returned to re-inspect it all over again.

We put her actions down to curiosity, but later there was reason to re-think that assessment.

When the calf was an hour old Kivy had it following

her at a wobbly gallop. It looked like a miniature black bear as it pushed its way through tall grass answering the cow's low guttural growls with a chorus of blats and bleats.

Not until Kivy had her calf as far from the birthing spot as the paddock would permit did she stop to let it explore hungrily around her for food. It wasn't having any success and knowing how well hidden the cow's bag is, we wondered how the calf would ever find a teat in amongst all that long hair.

Two-day old

Suddenly, as if out of patience with the bumbling of her offspring, Kivy turned her head and pushed the little creature under her belly, its head facing her hind legs. Then she squatted, and all but shoved a teat into an exploring mouth.

Within seconds greedy sucking sounds told us the calf, hidden under its mother's belly, had life giving food, warmth and protection. It should be OK now.

Before another day passed we weren't so sure.

It was June llth. Clarence anxious to spend time watching the calf, had given Kivy her grain, then taken his own mid-morning snack into the musk-ox paddock and sat down beside her to eat it.

The calf peeping out from between the cow's front legs eyed him warily at first, then walked slowly towards him. In minutes a tiny hoof was pawing at his pant leg. The calf seemed to want to climb up onto his knee. She was eyeing the water cup in his hand with what looked like interest, so he held it out to her thinking, "You're a curious one, for only a day old."

The next moment his eyes popped.

She was DRINKING! Actually drinking!

Day old ranch babies never drink water. It's unheard of. It simply IS NOT DONE. They don't even know how to drink. Even when they are older they splutter and slobber and slurp before they learn to drink properly.

When the water was gone Esky backed away. Clarence watched her go filled with foreboding.

A calf drinking like that could only mean one thing. The mother didn't have any milk. Yet when the calf popped beneath Kivy all the signs said it was nursing. The contented wagging of the tiny stub tail, the unmistakable sucking sounds, the dreamy, maternal look in Kivy's eyes as she semi-crouched above her offspring. And yet the little animal had been thirsty.

"Why not weigh Esky?" I suggested when Clarence came in, his face etched with misgivings. "If she's gaining you'll know she's getting milk."

Drinking from a tin

The bathroom scales recorded the calf's weight at twenty pounds. Before a week was over she had gained six more. That certainly wasn't made on just water. Obviously Kivy had milk, good rich milk. Clarence felt as if a stone had been lifted from around his neck.

That experience suggested to us musk-ox milk is so concentrated it satisfies hunger in seconds, (Esky rarely nursed for more than four or five seconds at a time) but not thirst. She needed water too to give her body the fluids it required, and she drank it in varying amounts every day.

Weighing Esky on a scale

* * *

Clarence had expected Kivy to be fiercely protective of her calf. She would have been had I or strangers tried to go near it, but she accepted my husband with absolute trust. He could pick up the calf, and although it always protested in a series of loud blats, Kivy ignored its cry for help. But there came a day when I was sure he had gone too far.

Kivy was feeding well back in the paddock when visitors came to see the calf. So Clarence picked up the little animal and carried it to the fence to show them. Just as he reached the fence a yappy little dog, that was supposed to have been left shut in a car, came streaking towards its owners, gleefully leaping into the air, its barks more strident than the ringing of a telephone inside a tin barrel. Everyone froze. Except Kivy.

She snorted and charged towards the only object within reach—the man holding her calf.

I felt mind-numbing fear. There wasn't a thing I could do but watch a tragedy happen.

When it seemed certain Kivy would plow into Clarence he spoke to her and held out his free hand. She slammed to a stop, sniffing anxiously at her offspring. Then she was off again, this time hurtling along the fence to get at the noisy dog whose shame-faced owners were quickly hustling him back to where he belonged.

Squinting against the scorching glare of the sun I turned to my husband who looked as if nothing untoward had happened, while I felt as if I had just been filtered through a sieve.

"It helps to be a bit crazy," I murmured "but please don't try that again. I couldn't stand it." His smile was soft and reassuring. But there was a hint of vulnerability in it too. He really hadn't been sure what Kivy would do.

* * *

Esky, the calf was almost a month old when a man from Fish and Wild Life came asking permission to take pictures of our musk oxen.

"No problem" I told him. "They're right here in the paddock" and I walked with him to where I had just fed them corn stalks. Kivy kept on eating, not at all concerned there was a stranger looking at her calf.

However this unconcern vanished like dry leaves swept up by a hurricane the moment he raised his camera.

Esky

She backed, snorted, stamped. Then charged at the man behind the fence with such vitriolic furry he tripped over his own feet in his haste to get away. She looked so dangerous he didn't feel safe even with a heavy guard rail, and a high fence, between them.

When Kivy went back to eating, his courage returned and he began edging closer. He still hoped for pictures.

As long as he was content to just stand and look he could rest his hand on the fence and Kivy ignored him, but when he raised his camera she flew at him like a belligerent buffalo.

We couldn't explain her behavior unless some long

dormant instinct was warning her that in the past men raising black things to their eyes had brought death to musk oxen. And sadly enough, they would again.

Esky and calf

Chapter Thirty Four

Sandy's Attack on Clarence

The day Esky was born Sandy pulled a Pearl Harbor. He might have killed my husband if a crow bar hadn't been within easy reach.

The bull had been prowling up and down his side of the paddock all day, periodically venting his venom on the recycled power poles that re-enforced the plank fencing at charge-level. I had joked to Clarence "Sandy's like any anxious father. Well . . ., maybe overdoing it a bit." But no one paid him much attention. The spotlight was on Kivy.

Sandy had been on choir-boy behavior since the rut had ended last fall, so that evening when my husband opened a gate for the bull to come in for water he didn't expect to be attacked

Without any warning Sandy's frustration boiled over like a pot of saskatoon jelly on a red-hot burner. He came for Clarence at a sizzling charge.

Luckily there was a fence for my husband to swing up on but he wasn't fast enough. Sandy caught his leg a wallop that sent red-hot pains shooting up it. Initially he thought it was broken. Though the pain persisted Clarence soon realized the leg wasn't broken, but that Sandy, still charging, had cracked the fence-protective power pole below him. With that smashed how long could the plank fencing last? The immensity of his danger was beginning to register. The bull had him trapped.

Suddenly his saw a long-forgotten crowbar leaning against the next fence panel. By shifting a little he could reach it. Next time Sandy charged he would be ready for him.

A couple of clouts with the crowbar took the fight out of Sandy. Clarence was eventually able to climb down and get away safely.

Afterwards if Sandy showed signs of getting dangerous again Clarence only had to show him the crow-bar, and he'd back off meek as milk. Yet out in the pasture he'd stalk around looking for trouble and in a hurry to meet it.

Clarence hated to admit it. But his pet bull had become dangerous. If he broke out as he had last summer how would we get him back?

Chapter Thirty Five

Lost Musk Oxen

Clarence was stacking hay, hoping to get another stack up before dark when a neighbor, Hughie Cooper, came to the door with a peculiar grin on his face, "D'ya wanna buy a musk ox?"

"A musk ox!? Are ours out?" My heart plummeted all the way down to my toes.

"Yeah. Your bull's with my cattle."

"Good Grief! We'll get him back. Right away." I didn't feel nearly as confident as I tried to sound. I felt sick.

"No hurry. He's not doing any harm. Just thought you'd like to know." and with that Hughie was off.

I gunned the pick-up to get Clarence and together we drove the three miles to Hughie's pasture. Once there it was easy to locate his cows. They were in a huddle around Sandy who was strutting and posturing, looking as puffed up with his own importance as a titillated toad. *No need to act so dammed smug,* I thought. *You'll never be their Lothario.*

"Come Sandy." Clarence was in the back of the pick-up now with a pan of oats in his hand. I drove slowly, and for the first half mile Sandy followed.

Then he started veering to the north. Even though he'd swing back each time Clarence walked up to him with the oats, he was tired of following and ready to look for some new adventure.

We weren't getting any closer to home, the oats were nearly gone, it was too dark to see. We'd had no choice but to give it up until morning.

Driving home alongside the musk-ox pasture the headlights picked out something we hadn't noticed on the way out.

A section of link-wire fence looked as if an army tank had torn through it. We tried to stretch the wire back into some semblance of a fence hoping if the fillies or Kivy wandered that way in the dark, they wouldn't realize it was no longer a secure fence. While working on the wire we heard what sounded like the bellow of a range bull looking for sex. It seemed to come from the musk-ox pasture. But that was impossible. There were no cattle in there. Not even close to it. We must have been mistaken.

That night I tossed and worried more than I slept. Clarence planned to take the stock trailer in the morning. There seemed a good chance Sandy would walk into it for oats. But what if he didn't . . .?

Maybe Rod and I should take our horses and drive him home? When said fast it sounded simple . . . except musk oxen are hard to drive. They'd rather stand and fight. Our horses had never worked musk oxen. Nor had we. And I wasn't hankering to start now.

When morning finally came Clarence left with the stock trailer and a good supply of oats. Rod and I followed. He on Eldorado, an Arabian gelding with lots of cow savvy, and I on Fantasy, a grey three-year-old mare who looked elegant but had little cattle experience.

We kept our horses to a walk to give the stock-trailer time to get to Sandy first. If he was going to go into the trailer there was a better chance he'd do it without us there.

Passing the musk-ox pasture we kept watching for Kivy. We didn't see her. She was probably over a hill or in a bush.

Meanwhile Clarence had found Sandy back with

Hughie's cows again. The bull came as soon as he was called. He even put his front feet up into the trailer. But after snatching a mouthful of oats he backed out, and no amount of coaxing could get him to step in again.

Rod Burpee on Gango Eldorado, the only horse known to have ever successfully herded musk oxen

When we arrived Clarence was ready to let us see what we could do. He drove ahead calling Sandy, stopping often to give him a taste of oats. At first we found by staying well back when Sandy was moving, but trotting up briskly, waving our ropes when he stopped, he'd turn and follow the truck and stock-trailer again. But near the spot where he had wanted to swing north the night before his willingness to co-operate vanished. He became obsessed with either running back, or heading north.

The horses had no trouble out-running him, but when they did he'd jolt to a stop, face them, head down snorting defiance. If we crowded him now he'd charge. If we didn't he had us beat. I began wishing I was somewhere else.

Rod, his face grim, shook out his lasso and twirled it within inches of the musk ox. Sandy stood his ground, snorting and stamping. He looked as big as a bull elephant and twice as dangerous.

Fantasy, a little behind and to one side of the gelding, watched with ears pricked and nostrils flaring. Eldorado seemed unconcerned when Rod stepped him closer. I froze in the saddle. Icy chills were stiffening my spine as I held my rope ready in case Sandy charged. It didn't help knowing I couldn't lasso a fence post at six feet.

Roping Sandy was the last thing Rod wanted to do, but he knew Sandy didn't like being caught. He was gambling on that. The boy kept the rope twirling closer and closer to the bull's head until it got too much for Sandy and he whirled and galloped towards Clarence's outfit. Rod had won that round.

Sandy still tried to cut back, but now the rope whistling around his head soon sent him stamping towards the truck and trailer again. When we got him out of the cattle-pasture and onto an unused road, we relaxed. From now on it should be easy.

We were talking quietly when Rod suddenly checked his gelding so abruptly it startled me.

"Hey Mum! Look!" Rod's voice was shrill with surprise. "Isn't that another musk ox?"

My eyes followed his out-flung arm and away to the north I saw what indeed did look like another musk ox.

"Holy Smoke!" Rod ejaculated "It's Kivy! "How

d'you suppose she got 'way up there?"

"I don't know." My voice sounded strange "But that's why Sandy keeps wanting to go north. He knows she's there."

"There's no sense taking him home until we get her too. You and Dad keep him here where she can see him. I'll ride up and let the fence down and try to get her across." Kivy, who had been running along a fence, had already disappeared from sight.

Not wanting to ride through a neighbour's field of grain Rod turned and went galloping back the way we had come. In moments he too was lost from sight. I could hear the drumming of the gelding's hooves fading into the distance. But although I kept watching, hoping to see either Kivy or Eldorado, there was nothing except the field of gently waving wheat framed by distant trees, and above a lonely hawk lazily hitching lifts on thermal up-drafts.

Fantsy tossed her head impatiently from time to time. Sandy, busy nipping off buck-brush berries, was in no hurry to go anywhere. Suddenly the mare's ears flew up and she whinnied. From not far away came an answering whinny. The next moment Eldorado trotted into sight.

"Where's Kivy?" I called.

"Dunna. Didn't see a sign of her. But I let the fence down anyway. You haven't seen her either?" There was disappointment in his voice.

Clarence left the truck and came to join us. Just as we were deciding we should split and ride separate directions around the field, leaving Clarence to stay with Sandy, he exclaimed. "There she is!"

It was indeed Kivy. She had popped up almost at our feet.

Now all we had to do was get her through the fence and take the two musk oxen down the road to home.

There was a gate a few feet from Sandy so it was no trouble to coax Kivy through it and shut it behind her.

In minutes we were on the move again, Clarence still ahead with the truck and trailer, Rod and I riding behind.

"Darn lucky to get her back that easy." Rod swung one leg up and hooked his knee over the saddle horn.

"Yeah, we could've had real tr—" I never finished because Sandy gave a sudden snort and tore after Kivy who swerved off the road and went crashing into some bushes. There was the screeching twang of stretching barbed wire, and Kivy was back through the fence again. Sandy stopped, and looking rather pleased with himself began eating leaves.

This time there was no gate close by, so Clarence had to let the fence down, then try to persuade Kivy to step over it. That was something she wasn't sure she wanted to do until Sandy moved further away.

We finally got underway again. But almost immediately Sandy took another dive at Kivy. She went crashing through another fence. This time it took longer to get her back.

"Heck!" growled Rod. "We'll never get them home this way. You stay behind them Mum. I'm gonna ride alongside that fence. When he chases her I'll try to keep her headed straight down the road."

Rod kept Eldorado between Kivy and the fence. When she walked he walked. When Sandy chased her and she took off like a frightened rabbit, Rod took off too, shouting like a hockey parent in the final seconds of a close game. Eldorado skimmed through ditches, leaped rocks, swerved around trees, jumped deadfall.

I thought Sandy began to look a little perplexed, as he snorted along behind. But perplexed or not we were making miles now. On the other side of the next little hill a gate opened into our land, and from there it was only half a mile to the home paddock.

Suddenly the stock-trailer, already at the top of the hill, slowed, then stopped. Clarence, out of the truck now, seemed to be waving, signalling to someone. What was going on?

As we stared open-mouthed a big silage-truck breasted the hill, seemed to falter, then quickly backed out of sight.

Rod turned and yelled back at me. "Watch them Mum. They might try to run back." My legs involuntarily tightened and Fantasy pranced a little.

The silage-truck had backed just beyond our gate so there was no need to try and crowd the musk ox past it, and so give Sandy another chance to chase Kivy through the fence.

The truck driver's eyes stuck out like mushrooms on a collection plate. Musk oxen aren't something one expects to meet . . . even on lonely roads. I grinned wishing I could hear the story he'd tell that evening.

Within minutes we had the musk oxen through the gate. Now their east boundary was our musk-ox fence, link-wire and foolproof. Or so we had thought until yesterday. Ahead and to the right was an open field. We relaxed again and Rod patting Eldorado grinned at me. "It would take a lot of money to buy him today Mum."

"He did OK didn't he," then I added cautiously, "But we aren't home yet. There's more bush and barbed wire ahead." The musk ox seemed to know this too for as soon as we had them beyond the link-wire fence they sailed off at a bouncing gallop, each heading in a different direction.

"I'll get Kivy," I yelled, but I doubt Rod heard me. Eldorado was already thundering after Sandy. Fantasy quickly showed she too might have the making of a competent musk-ox horse. I had to grab the saddle horn when she headed Kivy.

The rest of the way home the musk oxen handled like

old milk cows. We weren't sure if this was because they were tired, or if they were learning to respect a stock horse.

Later when we went back to do a proper repair job on the damaged link-wire we found a renegade Charolais bull in our musk-ox pasture. It was he who had wrecked the fence, but whether it was done fighting Sandy or out of sheer cussedness we'd never know. However knowing the musk ox hadn't done it made Clarence feel better about putting them back in their pasture.

That had happened the previous summer. Since then Sandy had become dangerous.

Chapter 36

"No Trespassing"

An August sun pounded the heat-cracked soil, blistered cucumber vines, cowered lettuce leaves, wilted dahlias. It was a great day for killing weeds. Now that Sandy was not stalking the paddock fence alongside me with hate in his eyes, hoeing was almost pleasant.

The bull's constant strutting and posturing, the pre-rut cussedness that kept him imprisoned in a state of perennial belligerence still bothered me . . . even knowing there was the added protection of iron guard rails on the inside of the paddock fence bordering my garden. However, now that Sandy, Kivy and the calf Esky were off by themselves, in a newly-fenced field connecting pasture to paddock, gardening was relaxing again.

Suddenly Rev who had been dozing at the edge of the garden was snarling beside me. The growls exposing her sharp white teeth sounded ominous. The glitter in her eyes dangerous. The tiny hairs along my spine bristled like the hackles on her neck

Two men were walking towards me. Not via the road, the normal way for anyone to come in, but from the direction of the barns and corrals. Beyond those there was nothing but miles of fields, range land AND the musk-ox pasture. No one had any right to be there. They were trespassers. Anger hardened my expression.

Didn't they know that ranchers and farmers view trespassers the way barbecue families view meandering skunks. And why was one of them carrying a wand-like pipe? The other had a queer looking black box contraption strapped to his shoulders? My hand involuntarily tightened around the hoe handle as I moved to intercept them. Rev, growling deep in her throat, stayed at my side.

The trespassers' clothes were rough and nondescript. The scraggly stubble darkening their faces suggested they had lost their razors. Their shoulder-length hair, lank and unkept, would have challenged a barber. They were young, perhaps only teen-agers, but they looked hard as nails.

"Where did you guys come from?" I demanded making no attempt to keep the edge of anger from my voice.

Instead of replying the taller of the two, a dark chap with a pronounced French accent shot out a question juxtaposed with fright. "Are those your buffalo? They almost got us."

"Buffalo? What buffalo?" I demanded in a voice high with surprise. But that dropped a key or two as a wave of understanding washed over me. "You mean musk oxen?" Then as the significance of what he had said sank in I seemed to be floundering in a rising wave of panic. It was necessary to get my heart and voice untangled before I could squeak "Are they out?"

"See! What did I tell you? They weren't buffalo." The chap with the blonde hair turned to his companion with a sickly grimace that may have been meant for a smile.

"But are they out?" I was almost shouting now.

"No . . . Well . . . I don't think so." The French lad seemed vague.

"Then what do you mean, 'They almost got you'? Where you in their pasture?" White hot anger boiled up in my veins. No one, absolutely no one, had any business in the musk-ox pasture.

Gradually the story came out.

The boys, for they were scarcely more, were employed by the Gas Co-Operative to walk the pipe-line carrying a pipe horn to locate the line and a sniffer to detect any possible gas-leakage along the route

They had been warned bears were dangerous and to wear bells in bear country. But this wasn't bear country. Setting out from Provost that morning they hadn't expected to encounter any animals except maybe the odd coyote or deer, and the occasional herd of range cattle, which their boss assured them wouldn't give them any trouble.

These Toronto and Montreal urbanites hadn't anticipated meeting anything to worry about on this stretch of pipe-line. Except hungry mosquitoes. They were well fortified with insect repellents.

The pipe-line crossing our property runs for half a mile along the south side of our musk-ox pasture. A pasture that was empty just now except for Terry Lee's stallion, Image, and his mares and foals. Then the pipeline angles west across the newly-fenced paddock connecting musk-ox pasture to home paddock.

"Jeez! That's the fence I'd like if I had horses," Bill (the blonde) had remarked when Image, always friendly, came galloping over to the fence accompanied by his Arabian mares and foals. After eating the alfalfa the boys pushed through the fence to them, Image and his harem moved off. And the young men continued on their way.

Before long they reached a second link-wire fence. This one was even higher than the first.

"Ye Gods! Folks around here sure believe in good fences. They must have awfully valuable horses. Gimmee that map. It's time for a look-see." When they realized the gas-line cut diagonally across the pasture ahead they stared at the fence with growing apprehension. "Hell! Are we supposed to climb over THAT. And lug this damn sniffer and pipe horn over too?"

"Naw. There's a gate. Just back there." Retracing

their steps they were soon following their route again. Half way into the pasture they stopped. "Hey! What was THAT?" A stamp reverberating through the silence sounded loud and ominous even to city folk whose knowledge of livestock is limited to their house cat. It came again. This time it sounded chilling. And frightening.

"God! There's buffalo in that bush. And I don't think they like us. I'm getting out of here. Come on." Bill lit out for the fence running with every inch of his body.

The 'buffalo'

Bob hesitated. He had never seen buffalo. Except in a zoo. This seemed a good opportunity to have a closer look. However the belching avalanche of hair and hate sizzling towards him quickly changed his mind. He raced after Bill wishing he had jet engines on his feet.

The fence was only a short distance, but the heavy machine strapped to his shoulder was holding him back.

It didn't take a quick backwards glance to tell him the thudding terror behind him was close now. Very close.

"Drop it! It's your only chance!" Bill's scream, ragged with fear, affected Bob like the blast from a tropical hurricane.

He yanked at the shoulder strap, felt a weight drop from him, then leaped into the air in a blaze of screaming muscles and stretching tendons. A reaching hand making contact with a fence post helped give him the lift he needed to vault over the wire. He landed on the other side stumbling but still running. The fury behind him was billowing out the link wire even as he landed.

The boys, their faces ashen, moved well back from the fence before they felt safe in sinking exhausted to the ground. For the moment they were safe. What about their machine?

"God!" You won't get me going back in there. Not for a million dollars." Bob spoke with flat finality, his eyes glued to the animal swaggering menacingly up and down the fence, stopping frequently to give the wire a vicious bunt, testing it for a possible weak spot.

"Neither would I" muttered Bill glumly "But what if the Gas Company charges us for the sniffer.? There goes our summer wages. Maybe more. Those darn machines probably cost a mint."

"Yeah. I know."

Bill got his breath back before he spoke again. When he did it was through heat cracked lips, and almost as if he was talking to himself. "Maybe there is a way. You go back towards the gate. Stay close enough to the fence so the bull will follow you. When you've got him to where he can't see me, I'll poke a pole under the fence and try to hook the machine and drag it out." Bill's eyes were already assessing the deadfall in an adjacent grove of poplars.

"Maybe. But I dunno." Bob had an air of greyness about him. Even his voice sounded grey "What if the damn buffalo breaks out? Look at him. He's still attacking the fence." The Montreal lad dragged himself to his feet like a tired pack-mule facing a straight-up cliff.

When Bob walked back towards the gate, the "buffalo" his eyes inflamed with the torment of unappeased lust, swaggered alongside throwing periodic demonic bunts into the fence without a break in pace.

Now Bill could do his thing. But he better do it quickly. Lying flat on his stomach he worked with frenzied haste trying to work the pole under the wire, conscious all the time of a furious hammering in the region of his heart. A second "buffalo" was moving closer. Kivy was merely curious. She thought the black box looked worth investigating. However the boys didn't know that.

"Damn! The pole's not long enough. It won't quite reach." Bill stared at the pole with a look that said he expected to be momentarily executed. "But hey! If I jam my shoulder against the wire. And if it gives, even a little . . ." A moment later his shout rang high with success. "Yeah Bob! I've got it. It's out. Bob! Where are you? Are you OK?"

As the boys talked I resisted the impulse to berate them for their stupidity. They should never have gone into the musk-ox pasture. They could have been badly hurt. Or killed. But it wasn't their fault. Not really. They were only doing their job. It was the Pipe Line Company who needed the blast. And they got a double one.

Within a year the pipe line had been re-routed so it no longer crossed our musk-ox pasture.

When the Easterners heard their encounter had not been with buffalo, but with musk oxen, their eyes stood out like the Biblical burning bush blazing in an Alberta snowdrift. "You mean those animals are from wind-rimmed tundras in the high Arctic? Wow! Wait until I tell that to my folks back home. But I can promise you one thing. They're never going to believe it. Maybe we can come back and get some pictures." Then he shifted uneasily. "I'd want a tele-photo lens though."

After the pipe-line walkers had continued on their inspection walk I made "No Trespassing" signs with DANGER spelled out in big bold red letters. There must be no recurrence of today's foolishness.

Chapter Thirty Seven

Hollywood at Gango

It began with a phone call in July 1984. A man identifying himself as John Scott wanted to bring someone. . . , (my husband didn't catch the name) to see the musk ox. It had something to do with taking pictures. Maybe a lot of pictures. It sounded ho-hum. I was considerably less than enthusiastic.

My husband, who doesn't hear too well on the phone now, seemed vague as to who the men where or why they wanted a lot of pictures. I assumed they were from some television station wanting to do a clip about musk oxen. It had happened before. Clarence and his musk oxen were not unfamiliar to radio or TV audiences. I wished Clarence had told them to wait until after haying.

Ordinarily Clarence likes showing the musk oxen to anyone interested in them, especially if they phone ahead to set up an appointment. But this was July. It was haying time.

Maybe John Scott, whoever he was, would forget about our musk ox. I hoped he would.

Due to Clarence's worsening health he was having to slow down. Most of our land was sold. The musk oxen were to go too, as soon as harvest was over. They wouldn't be ours much longer.

A week later I answered the phone to hear, "Mrs. Burpee? John Scott here." The voice sounded pleasant. "Jack Couffer has flown in from Vancouver. I'd like to bring him down this afternoon to see the musk ox, if that's OK."

"Well, it isn't" I snapped. "You can't come today. Clarence is too busy to show anyone his musk ox."

Locating the herd in a patchwork of prairie wool, alfalfa fields, poplar bluffs and willow-ringed sloughs could take hours in the heat of the day when the animals are normally resting and too lethargic to respond immediately to Clarence's call.

"But Mrs. Burpee, Couffer flew out this morning especially to see the musk oxen." Now the tone implied that at the name "Couffer" I should automatically have fallen down and touched my forehead to the ground three times. I hadn't.

Still, I had to tell the man something. "If you want to see the musk oxen, be here at seven tomorrow morning." Having delivered that ultimation my forked tail lashed the floor with evil glee. Now we'd see how badly they wanted to see musk oxen. The ranch is a three-hour-plus drive from the city. Around here even the birds don't get up at 4 a.m.

"Good. Tell Clarence we'll be there at seven. Thanks for your help Mrs. Burpee."

The line clicked and I was left staring at the dead receiver. Ye Gods! Who were these men? What was their interest in musk oxen?

The next morning the mystery cleared.

A Hollywood movie company was filming *The Clan of the Cave Bear*, Jean M. Auel's International best seller about the customs, conflicts and loves of a band of Neanderthalls who hunt hairy mammoths. Hollywood wanted to substitute musk oxen, equally hairy, and virtually unchanged since the dawn of prehistoric man, for their hunt scenes.

Most of the filming would take place near Penticton, British Columbia, but both Scott and Couffer, if Clarence agreed, hoped to do the hunt shots in our musk-ox pasture.

Scott said our animals were the most impressive he'd ever seen, either in the wild or in zoos, and he was eager to use them. Couffer was more interested in the pasture's virgin prairie wool, ringed by poplar and willow bluffs. It afforded a setting pristine enough to catch the critical eye of a man who had cut his teeth filming Walt Disney's animal movies, then gone on to still higher acclaim after directing the wild life shots for Farley Mowatt's Never Cry Wolf.

Some of the actors: Kivy and Esky and their calves

Both men were anxious for permission to do the hunt scene at our ranch, the filming to start within a few days.

Clarence agreed they should get started right away too, but for a different reason. He didn't want anyone to get hurt. Equally important the musk oxen mustn't be hurt either. In another few weeks the bulls would be in rut and dangerously explosive. It would be too risky then for strangers to go into their pasture on foot. Later that day Clarence thrust anxious fingers through his hair, his tall figure seemed to stoop a little as though a weight was pressing on his mind. "I'm not sure how the musk oxen will react to being 'hunted.'"

As for me I wanted to rush to the party line and yell "Hey Folks! Guess what? There's a Hollywood film crew coming here. The day after tomorrow. Imagine! Holywood! Here! On our ranch!" That bit of information would have roared through the district like a prairie fire on a windy day. Within hours the entire community would be ablaze with excitement.

But Clarence, easing work-roughened fingers around the inside of his shirt collar as if it had suddenly become too tight, said tersely "Hold it. The less people who hear about this the better. There'll be enough going on to make the musk ox suspicious as it is. They don't need the distraction of noisy crowds lining the fences.

Couffer wanted Clarence with him during all the filming. I wasn't sure if this was for the protection of the film crew. Or to make sure the animals weren't harmed. Perhaps a bit of both.

While Clarence and Couffer were off plunging through bush and prairie wool to select the exact right spot to set up the filming blind, the grandchildren and I watched a four-hour make-up miracle that plummeted modern men back through the mist of antiquity to emerge as cave dwellers so prehistoric their ability to speak was only just starting to develop.

This picture was taken when Jack Couffer had his Hollywood crew at the ranch filming hunt scenes for the movie The Clan of the Cave Bear. Stuntmen John and Keith Wardlow are being made up to play the part of DROOG and CRUG. Jordie Thomson is to be the wolf-man. The man with the camera (extreme right) took frequent pictures during the make-up process. This was necessary so the cavemen always looked the same throughout the entire filming of the movie. The children watching are Bridget Currier, (in blue) and little Heather Degenhardt in red jeans.

Human actors

These hairy, chinless "flatheads" with skimpy loin clothes, wooden spears, and crouching gait more primate than Homo sapien, looked absurd against a backdrop of combines, tractors, and steel granaries. In among trees, prairie wool, and musk oxen they might not look quite so ridiculous.

When the blind had been set up, and Couffer was satisfied the hunters looked sufficiently dawn-age, he looked at his watch, glanced at the sun, studied the shadows, then announced "the light will be right in half an hour."

Within minutes a van left the yard. In it were the producer, the actors, and the camera men, along with Couffer and Clarence, plus John Scott, and Bruce Taylor, a local rancher with a good cattle dog. The vehicle moved cautiously around the perimeter of the musk-ox pasture to within easy walking distance of the blind. Then the occupants moved quietly, almost furtively, to whichever designated spot Couffer directed them.

Taylor and his dog stayed at the van. Having a dog on location was John Scott's brain child. A brain child he hadn't wanted to throw out even after Clarence had told him "dogs are a hazard around musk oxen." Scott found it hard to believe a dog, such as Bruce's, couldn't herd musk oxen as well as it did cattle. Clarence, supposing the dog wouldn't do any harm, provided it stayed out of sight, hadn't specifically forbidden it to come. There was always the possibility, although it seemed remote at this point, that if someone did get attacked the dog might distract the musk oxen long enough for that person to be dragged to safety.

The hunters carrying wooden spears and naked except for wispy loin clothes, skins on their feet and wolf pelts slung around their shoulders, hunkered down in the buckbrush and silver willow, hoping to totally submerge themselves into the landscape. The reputation of musk oxen is such that the stunt men who were to play the roll of hunters, had been training for the part for months. Yet an aura of tension hung over them as they waited for the musk oxen to appear.

Clarence walked off to call the musk oxen. He needed to bring them close to the hunters in such a way that when the flatheads sprang out of hiding all the action was within camera range. And he was not.

I had gone with the remainder of the movie people in the second van. It stopped just inside the pasture gate where we could watch and yet be out of range of the cameras.

When Clarence called the musk ox they would come to him, but he was having trouble getting them to follow him to where Couffer wanted them. They'd start, then turn and run stamping and snorting back to the bush they'd just left. And each time they ran back their suspicion seemed to grow a little. There were too many strange voices floating on the evening breeze.

The wardrobe and make-up people had clambered onto the roof of their van, and now they clung there like flies on a dead buffalo. They laughed, they talked, they swore. Every time anyone shifted position, or even swatted a mosquito, the roof twanged as if it had been hit by a rubber mallet. The smirks and snide remarks when the musk ox ran back suggested these people hadn't believed Couffer when he told them "when Burpee calls, the musk ox follow him." Now they felt justified in their skepticism.

Ye Gods! Don't these people know enough to keep quiet? Can't they see what they're doing to the musk oxen?

Finally in utter desperation I snorted "You guys better shut up. If you don't my husband is wasting his time out there. So is Couffer. And all the others. You better get this van the heck out of here. Go back to the yard. You can watch from there. You've got binoculars."

That outburst brought a condescending smirk from an ostentatious six-footer in a black cowboy hat who had assumed grandiose importance in his own eyes. As if HE had a special phone-line to God while I was the hairy brown caterpillar crawling on his boot. The rest kept on talking.

To hell with Hollywood and their stupidity. I'd walk back, get our truck, then pick up Clarence. I was worried about him. He'd been doing more walking than expected. That left him wide open for an insulin reaction. Being a brittle diabetic he gets almost no warning of them.

As I began stalking off Mr. Black Hat suddenly realized maybe God had flipped the switch on him. The worm had grown into something too big for him to step on. But he wasn't quite able to eliminate the imperious ring from his voice. "You can't take your truck out there. It would leave tracks."

My Irish hit the sky and bounced back double strength.

"I'll take the truck anywhere I damn well please. Whose pasture do you think this is?"

"Please wait Mrs. Burpee. "The tone was definitely conciliatory now. "There's no need for you to pick up your husband. I can see them (he lowered the binoculars as he spoke) and it looks as if they're all leaving the blind." He was right.

No footage was shot that evening.

The next day, Couffer, perhaps at Clarence's suggestion, issued an ultimatum. "Absolutely no one not needed at the film site is to set foot inside the musk-ox pasture. Understood?" But he asked me to go.

I wasn't sure if this was politic because he realized I'd probably go anyway, (and he couldn't stop me) or if he actually thought I might be helpful. When he asked if I'd mind taking our red pick-up truck and parking it just behind the blind, I said "sure." (I had planned on riding Fantasy to within easy watching distance anyway.)

Couffer was anxious there be nothing done to make the musk oxen suspicious today. Perhaps that was why he wanted our red half-ton parked near the blind. The musk ox consider it an old friend. Or was he, after seeing the demolition job the musk ox had done on the blind during the night, worried they might attack the repaired version with men and cameras inside? The truck might give a feeling of security to those crouching nervously inside the flimsy jute and lath fabrication, but it would be a false security.

I had no illusions about what would happen to a parked half-ton should the musk ox decide to vent their ire on it. I'd seen a bull charge a new pressure-treated seven-inch-diameter post and break it in one crack.

When leaving the blind the first evening Couffer suggested it be left in place. "So the musk ox can get used to seeing it and won't be frightened of it tomorrow."

Clarence had laughed. "Leave it up if you want. But be prepared to rebuild it tomorrow. The musk oxen aren't scared of it. They'll be tearing it apart as soon as we leave." And he was right. They had.

Couffer's "woman" had arrived that morning from Kenya and had asked to ride with me in the pick-up to watch the filming. I said "Sure. Glad to have you."

But when Couffer heard he said "No. Only Mary goes." His friend (she had a name I couldn't pronounce) looked as if disaster had blighted her life. I was sorry too. She was nice.

The sun was nearly at the right angle for filming. I had driven Clarence and Couffer down a tree-shaded trail that brought them out near the repaired blind. Couffer strode back to the van behind, ordering "I want absolute quiet. That means no slamming of vehicle doors," then he and

Clarence slipped away through the trees as silently as a pair of Indian.

Almost immediately my truck door, passenger side, opened and Crug, the cave men who in real life is Keith Wardlow, eased himself in beside me. As we talked in low whispers the only sound from those lounging outside was the slap of hands on bare flesh. The near-naked hunters had forgotten their can of OFF.

As soon as Couffer and Clarence had decided on the strategy for that day's filming they reappeared, and everyone moved to his designated place.

I watched the musk ox follow Clarence to where the Director wanted them. I saw the hunters leap out of hiding brandishing wooden spears and making meaningless guttural sounds, saw their camouflage of wolf-hides drop from naked bodies. The men ran at a crouching lope, sometimes springing up in a leap that reminded me of a lost dog trying to find its way out of a field of tall grain. I noticed too how assiduously the hunters avoided getting too close to their quarry. It was abundantly clear they had no desire to make the musk oxen feel pressured into whirling to defend themselves.

Time and time again Clarence called the musk oxen back, and they obliged by galloping away, snorting and stamping when the hunters sprang up around them. They seemed to enter into the spirit of the thing, willing, even eager, to return for a re-play when Clarence called them.

Couffer was pleased with that day's filming. He wanted to do more before the hunters had to return to B.C. for the scheduled filming of other scenes.

There was hay ready to stack again and Clarence was anxious to get at it. Walking the pasture with Couffer each afternoon to locate the musk oxen was taking too much of his time. Ordinarily when he wants the musk ox he drives out and calls and they come sauntering out of whatever bush they've been in.

But Couffer needed to know their precise location in relation to the blind, and then hope they didn't move until everything was ready for the "take" call. With his penchant for excellence it seemed vital he should know the exact angle the animals would be approaching the cameras.

It was important there be no vehicle tracks where the cameras could pick them up . . . wheels wouldn't be invented for a long time yet, . . . so when locating the musk oxen Clarence walked. He doesn't like riding. Whereas I do.

So? Why shouldn't I ride out and locate the musk oxen for Couffer? That would free Clarence's afternoons so he could keep on haying until it was time for him to call the musk oxen into position.

Several years ago we had made the mistake of pasturing musk oxen with horses. Kivy had learned to boss them. Now if one ventured too close to her she'd charge it at a snorting, hair-flapping, ground-jarring gallop. So I'd have to be careful. I'd ride Eldorado. He stands quietly when asked too.

"Here Mary. Take my walkie-talkie. Call me as soon as you find them."

I nodded to Jack Couffer and was turning to ride from the yard when John Scott called "Wait a minute. The walkie-talkie? Will it spook your horse?" Concern was adding creases to his wind-leathered face.

"I don't think so. He's sensible."

"Better try it before you go. A lot of horses fly to pieces if they aren't used to them." Scott, a movie stock supplier, looked as if his experience with horses and "on-location riders" had left him with a sour taste. However, he ran his hand down Eldorado's neck the way horsemen are prone to do when standing next a good animal, before striding quickly back to the movie van. The next moment his deep voice came crackling from my hand. Edlorado is too well adjusted to fly apart because an unknown voice comes booming out of the air just inches back of his ears. That made Scott look at the gelding with added respect.

It took an hour of cautious riding to locate the musk oxen. They were so well camouflaged among the trees I wouldn't have found them then if I hadn't whiffed the odour peculiar to bulls approaching rut. I supposed they'd seen me, but I hoped they were too lethargic to bother getting up to investigate.

I rode off some distance before speaking softly into the walkie-talkie. "I've found them. They're in the first bush west of the blind."

Couffer's voice booming back at me sounded as if he was trying to out-shout a bulldozer. "Well done Mary. We're almost ready to bring out the cameras. Can you hold the musk oxen where they are?"

"I don't know" I hissed. "Kivy is coming out of the bush right now. If she charges I'm leaving. And if you have to talk to me again whisper."

"Good Girl." He breathed that message so softly Eldorado didn't even twitch an ear. And Kivy who had been rubbing her nose, the forerunner of a charge, decided it was too much bother to chase a horse standing so quietly he could have been a shadow.

"Suddenly it hit me. Great Thundering Guns! I'd been giving orders to a Hollywood V.I.P. And he had taken them! I couldn't have been dreaming? Could I? No. A horse fly had just bitten me, and now another was biting the tender under-part of Eldorado's belly. No amount of muscle twitching, head swinging, tail swishing or feet stamping, could dislodge the insect. There was nothing for it but to slip off and kill it for him.

That brought Kivy stalking out of the bush again. Her

long hair swishing with studied intent, her stride both determined and malevolent.

I flew back into the saddle and rode further off, hoping she wouldn't bother to follow. She stopped as if considering whether it was worth the effort, then ambled back to the cool of the trees. Soon afterwards Clarence's truck and the movie van came through the link-wire gate.

Minutes later the familiar call "Come Kivy. Come Musk Oxen." rang through the pasture and I could hear the almost inaudible swish of hairy bodies brushing through undergrowth. Everything seemed to be going according to schedule.

Eldorado and I could relax. And listen.

Snorts and a ground-jarring gallop told me the hunters had once again sprung out of hiding. The calls "Come Musk Oxen" told me Clarence was bringing them back. But there were other sounds too. And from a different direction. Wild shouts. Spine tingling snorts. A thumping gallop. Voices I couldn't identify. What was going on? But nothing came over the walkie talkie. It couldn't be anything serious.

When the setting sun distorted shadows it was time to head home.

As people lounged around our truck and the movie vans, sharing experiences, drinking pop and nibbling chocolate bars, I sensed a feeling of camaraderie, despite our varied backgrounds.

I hadn't yet noticed anyone was missing.

I didn't until Scott's pick-up drove into the yard and three rather sheepish looking men got out, followed by a dog acting as disillusioned as a kicked cur. When Clarence heard what they had been up to the amusement that hovered momentarily in his eyes didn't match the grim set of his lips.

Scott had had a run in with Kivy that afternoon. He

had intended to head her back into camera range. Instead she had shown him how fast a man can clear a seven-foot high fence. But running away, jumping fences, weren't feats Scott, who saw himself as an experienced stockman, took kindly too. He had come away from it with an uncomfortable feeling of inadequacy, of not being in total control of the situation. And he intended to do something about it.

So he had asked Taylor and Couffer to stay back with him when everyone else left. He had been confident right from the first that Bruce's well-trained dog would have no trouble with musk oxen. Now he was anxious to prove it.

Bruce, realizing Clarence is a man who knows what he is talking about, took the precaution of eyeing nearby trees until he picked out one that looked big and solid enough to last a hundred years, before whistling his dog from the truck. Scott then drove the pick-up to where he and Couffer could watch without being a distraction to either dog or musk oxen.

When Taylor pointed towards the musk ox and said "fetch 'em in boy" the Border Collie loped off as if it was routine to bring in a herd of musk oxen. His tongue, moist and red, lolled confidently from a laughing mouth. The next moment the little animal was streaking back the way he had come with ten musk oxen snorting up his tail.

Bruce, a self-conscious grin playing feebly around his mouth, told Clarence afterwards "I got up that tree so fast I surprised myself. When your biggest bull smashed into it, and a poplar that had looked massive when I picked it out, swayed like a sapling, I began wishing I'd listened to you. I was sure if any one of the animals snorting around it gave it one more wallop the tree and I would both be history. The power those animals pack into a charge is mind bogling."

With Taylor up the tree, the dog sensing his only safe

haven was the truck, had streaked through the trees and flung himself into it. Then he'd hunkered down hoping to make himself invisible.

As soon as the dog was out of sight the musk oxen lost interest in the man up the tree. When they moved off he was able to climb down and make his way to the truck with his mind firmly made up on one point. He and his dog were wasting their time. Tomorrow he would be back haying.

The next day Couffer reluctantly gave permission for his "woman" to accompany him to the blind. In Kenya she keeps cheetahs and tigers as pets, yet she found the filming of the musk oxen "Absolutely fascinating."

There was a tinge of awe in her voice as she retold the experience. "We all sweat blood when a bull left the herd and swaggered close to the blind. I was sure he was sizing it up for immediate demolition but as soon as your husband called him he walked away like a trained dog. It's unreal the control Clarence has over those huge hairy animals. Most men would be scared spitless.

"Jack was so pleased with the close-ups the cameras were getting I didn't want move, or do anything to spoil it. So I crouched there like a chunk of rock, didn't even brush off the horsefly biting my arm."

"You mean you sat there. . . . And let a horsefly chew a chunk out of you? Ye Gods! How could you? Those things have jaws like red hot pincers."

She smiled. "Seeing the musk oxen come that close was so fascinating the bite seemed trivial"

Now it was my turn to be impressed.

* * *

I was becoming concerned for Clarence's safety. The rut was getting closer. What if the bulls' natural aggression at this time of the year was speeded up by the dog, or by having people leap out of hiding to scare them?

Clarence, nearing seventy, on foot, with ten musk ox following him, would be a sitting duck if the animals got riled up and charged him. But having been born without a scare-button he brushed my fears aside "I'll be all right. I always try to keep Kivy between me and the bulls. They won't bother her." Never-the-less we both knew there was danger. And I remembered Sandy.

As a concession to my fears there would now be three riders, out of sight, but close, when filming was in progress. If an animal turned ugly we planned to come charging in at converging angles and hope the momentum of our charge coupled with enough hollering to blister war paint off an Indian, would startle the musk oxen and send them scampering back to the bush. The element of surprise would be vital, otherwise the musk ox would attack the horses.

Although our adrenaline never completely switched off we had no rescue calls. Nor were we sorry we only had to sit and wait and swat mosquitoes.

When the time came for "Hollywood" to return to their mountain top location near Penticton, most of the folks told us they had enjoyed their time at the ranch and were looking forward to seeing us again in a couple of weeks.

I had mixed feelings about saying goodbye. Having a bit of Hollywood on the ranch had been largely a fun experience. But I wasn't sure I wanted them back. The next time around the bulls would be closer to the rut.

However, I needn't have worried. Within a week Couffer came back to tell us he had severed relations with the company filming *Clan of the Cave Bear*. Someone else would be taking over from him. That meant by the time the new director was ready to start filming the bulls would be in full rut, and deadly. We wanted no part in something were people were sure to get hurt.

A pending deal to sell the musk oxen was finalized. They became someone else's responsibility. They went to a rancher in northern Alberta, who Clarence believed would give them the same care and understanding he had given them.

Chapter Thirty Eight

Afterword

Years have passed since Clarence began striding towards a dream—the eventual domestication of musk oxen.

Esky and her calf

Sometimes he stumbled. Sometimes he walked boldly. Sometimes he seemed to be groping in the dark for a light switch that always eluded his touch. He was constantly grappling with the onion bulb of trial and error, peeling away the old skin, exposing the new. New challenges. New experiences. New problems. Sometimes heart-warming success.

Clarence holds a treat up for Sandy

Sometimes I was sure we must both be a bit crazy to have dared tackle such an enormous project on our own.

Yet Clarence proved to his own satisfaction that musk oxen do have potential as domestic animals.

We learned young musk oxen can be tamed. When

tamed they are often easier to handle than range cows. Their grazing habits benefit run-down pastures. They control the spread of unwanted brush and weeds unpalatable to bovine herds. They adapt well to our Alberta climate. There is a brisk demand for qiviut among hobby spinners and knitters. Musk oxen often show remarkable intelligence. Some display a sense of humour. They are full of surprises.

Yet despite these plusses our venture into musk oxen was not the success my husband had hoped for.

Part of a herd of eleven musk oxen at Gango

This was largely due to Government restrictions. Restrictions that denied us the opportunity to obtain a much-needed gene bank of calves from the Arctic . . . some of which, without human intervention, were doomed to die of starvation in the frigid cold of a tundra winter.

Closer to home Provincial restrictions controlled game farms and what could be done with the animals raised on them. (I understand that restriction has now been removed.) Our only outlet for surplus bulls was other game farms. Most game farms wanted a breeding pair which we couldn't supply because our cows outdid themselves producing male calves. However if the North West Territories had waived restrictions on selling live calves (it seemed OK for them to die of starvation, or be shot in the name of research) others interested in musk oxen as farm animals could have paired our tame bulls with wild caught heifers and been one step ahead on the road to domestication.

Another piece of Government red tape forbade the sale of musk-ox meat in Alberta. We could have butchered animals for our own use. But we don't eat our friends. So while there were musk oxen on the ranch for fourteen years, we never tasted their meat. It wouldn't be until many years later that I was served musk-ox meat at Resolute on Cornwallis Island in the high Arctic. It was from an old trophy bull. The taste and flavour was about what one would expect from a Hereford monarch.

If Clarence's dream of seeing musk oxen grazing on ranches throughout the country is to become reality, it is vital, in my opinion, that not only should the meat become a marketable commodity but it must become possible to replace musk-ox bulls after each year's rut with younger, less aggressive males. I understand this is often done with Billy goats.

This would make handling them safer and it would eliminate broken corral rails, snapped off fence posts. When a mature bull charges into anything, be it tree, rail or post, his idea of play is lethal for his target. Macho males seem to see it as a personal challenge to crack whatever they hit at the first wallop. If they don't they keep on charging.

In the spring of 1981, wild herds on some Arctic islands had grown so large Government Wise Men decreed something must be done about it.

That "something" was to send out men on skidoos and in the name of "research" drive more than two hundred musk oxen to the outskirts of camp to be shot. Everything was killed. Even day-old calves. I could have cried. What wouldn't we have given for a chance to save the babies and bring a new gene bank into our herd?

The spring of 1982 saw a similar massacre. This time thirteen calves were spared so the veterinary College at Saskatoon could study various aspects of musk oxen, but not, unfortunately, their value as domestic animals.

Perhaps some day men of real vision will make it possible for northerners to establish a gene pool from which serious breeders could select for the qualities they want. Only then can the domestication of musk oxen become a reality.

When that comes about musk oxen will give the world of fashion a wool with the elegance of mink and ermine. Qiviut will fill the needs of those who on principle refuse to wear fur yet want the exotic luxury of fine clothes. However to harvest qiviut the musk oxen must be manageable. Which means domestication.

Despite the frustrations over red tape, the almost complete lack of replacement stock, my husband never regretted picking up the gauntlet of challenge. He made a lot of progress with animals about which so little was known some people still think of them as near mythical survivors of the last ice-age. Whereas they are merely animals who escaped total annihilation at the hands of hunters by becoming wild and wary in an inhospitable land of scanty food and bone chilling cold.

I believe someday the torch my husband lit so many years ago to light the way towards musk-ox domestication will blaze up again and ignite the fires of interest in other hearts.

"To you from failing hands we throw the torch."

Clarence and Sandy